AUCKLAND & THE BAY OF ISLANDS

ROAD TRIPS

This edition written and researched by

Brett Atkinson and Peter Dragicevich

HOW TO USE THIS BOOK

Reviews

In the Destinations section:

All reviews are ordered in our authors' preference, starting with their most preferred option. Additionally:

Sights are arranged in the geographic order that we suggest you visit them and, within this order, by author preference.

Eating and Sleeping reviews are ordered by price range (budget, midrange, top end) and, within these ranges, by author preference.

Map Legend

Routes

▨ Trip Route
▨ Trip Detour
▨ Linked Trip
▨ Walk Route
Tollway
Freeway
Primary
Secondary
Tertiary
Lane
Unsealed Road
Plaza/Mall
Steps
)= = Tunnel
Pedestrian
Overpass
--- Walk Track/Path

Boundaries
--- International
--- State/Province
—— Cliff

Hydrography
River/Creek
Intermittent River
Swamp/Mangrove
Canal
Water
Dry/Salt/
Intermittent Lake
Glacier

Highway Markers
① Highway Marker

Trips
1 Trip Numbers
9 Trip Stop
Walking tour
Trip Detour

Population
✪ Capital (National)
◉ Capital (State/Province)
● City/Large Town
○ Town/Village

Areas
Beach
Cemetery (Christian)
Cemetery (Other)
Park
Forest
Reservation
Urban Area
Sportsground

Transport
✈ Airport
Cable Car/ Funicular
Ⓟ Parking
Train/Railway
Tram

Note: Not all symbols displayed above appear on the maps in this book

Symbols In This Book

✓ Top Tips
🔗 Link Your Trips
💬 Tips from Locals
➤ Trip Detour
📖 History & Culture
👪 Family

🍷 Food & Drink
🌳 Outdoors
📷 Essential Photo
🏃 Walking Tour
🍴 Eating
🛏 Sleeping

◉ Sights
🏖 Beaches
🏃 Activities
🎓 Courses
☞ Tours
✦ Festivals & Events

🛏 Sleeping
🍴 Eating
🍸 Drinking
☆ Entertainment
🛍 Shopping
ⓘ Information & Transport

These symbols and abbreviations give vital information for each listing:

🕿 Telephone number
🕙 Opening hours
🅿 Parking
🚭 Nonsmoking
❄ Air-conditioning
@ Internet access
🛜 Wi-fi access
🏊 Swimming pool
🥗 Vegetarian selection
🍴 English-language menu
👪 Family-friendly

🐾 Pet-friendly
🚌 Bus
⛴ Ferry
🚃 Tram
🚆 Train
apt apartments
d double rooms
dm dorm beds
q quad rooms
r rooms
s single rooms
ste suites
tr triple rooms
tw twin rooms

CONTENTS

3

Above Bay of Islands

WELCOME TO
AUCKLAND & THE BAY OF ISLANDS

Reluctantly leave Auckland's harbour-fringed urban charms and chart a path north to sleepy harbours, compact coves and destinations etched into this young nation's heritage.

The Bay of Islands combines natural beauty with Māori and colonial history and further north is windswept and spiritual Cape Reinga. The upper west coast of New Zealand's North Island is less developed but equally spectacular, and Auckland is the perfect base for journeys combining fine wine, farmers markets and local wildlife.

Just a short drive away, the stunning Coromandel Peninsula is fringed by some of NZ's finest beaches and most spectacular coastal road trips.

AUCKLAND & THE BAY OF ISLANDS

1 Northland & the Bay of Islands
Coastal scenery, Māori culture and NZ history all combine on this northern odyssey.

6–8 DAYS

SOUTH PACIFIC OCEAN

TASMAN SEA

Mokohinau Islands

Hen & Chicken Islands

Poor Knights Islands

Cavalli Islands

Cape Reinga
Te Paki
Waitiki Landing
Te Kao
North Cape
Ngataki
Waihopo
Pukenui
Motutangi
Waiharara
Awanui
Kaitaia
Ahipara
Herekino
Warawara Forest
Karikari Peninsula
Doubtless Bay
Great Exhibition Bay
Taipa
Mangonui
Whangaroa
Kaeo
Matauri Bay
Whangaroa Harbour
Puketi Forest
Omahuta Forest
Kerikeri
Puketona
Pakaraka
Paihia
Russell
Waitaka
Russell Forest
Oakura
Helena Bay
Whakapara
Hikurangi
Matapouri
Ngunguru
Whangarei
Ruakaka
Uretiti
Waipu
Langs
Kaikohe
Taheke
Rawene
Omapere
Opononi
Hokianga Harbour
Waipoua State Forest
Maunganui Bluff (460m)
Kaihu
Maropiu
Baylys Beach
Dargaville
Tangowahine
Waimakariri River
Mangakahia River
Cape Brett
Bay of Islands

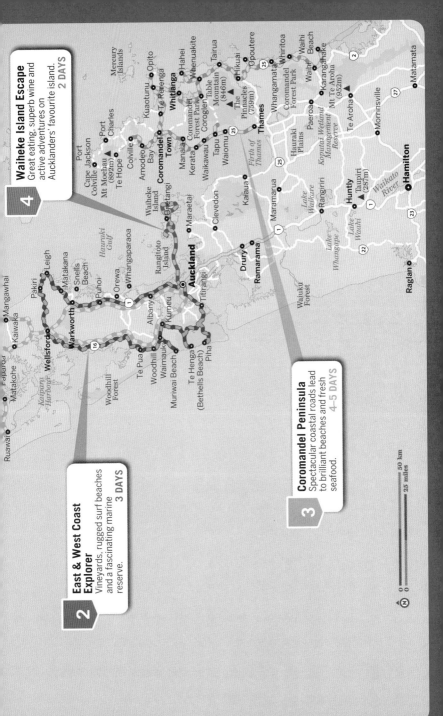

Waiheke Island Escape
Great eating, superb wine and active adventures on Aucklanders' favourite island.
2 DAYS

4

East & West Coast Explorer
Vineyards, rugged surf beaches and a fascinating marine reserve.
3 DAYS

2

Coromandel Peninsula
Spectacular coastal roads lead to brilliant beaches and fresh seafood.
4–5 DAYS

3

50 km

25 miles

AUCKLAND & THE BAY OF ISLANDS

HIGHLIGHTS

★

Waiheke Island (left) The welcome sign reads 'Slow Down. You're Here', and most visitors quickly oblige. Rural roads meander to sophisticated vineyard restaurants with stellar views back to Auckland. See it on Trip 4

Auckland (above) Auckland's Edwardian baroque Ferry Building sits grandly along the city's vibrant waterfront. See it on Trips 1 2 4

Bay of Islands (right) Enjoy walking trails that offer bird-watching and breathtaking coastal views. See it on Trip 4

CITY GUIDE

AUCKLAND

Arrayed around two natural harbours, Auckland celebrates a maritime vibe with waterfront restaurants and bars, and exciting ways to explore nearby islands and beaches. Observe Auckland's ocean-fringed horizons from the Sky Tower, head to Waiheke Island for a vineyard lunch, or learn about Kiwi culture at the Auckland Museum.

Getting Around

Auckland traffic is busy and parking expensive, so use the Link bus network instead. The Red City Link ($1) shuttles around the city centre, while the Green Inner Link ($2.50) services SkyCity, Ponsonby and the Auckland Museum.

Parking

Street parking options and car parks dot the city centre, costing up to $13 per hour. Park at the Wynyard Quarter car park (entrance on Beaumont St), where the first hour is free and each additional hour is $2. From there catch the City Link bus.

Above Auckland city and harbour at dawn

Where to Eat

Head to the harbour-front Wynyard Quarter for good restaurants. The nearby Britomart Precinct features eateries in repurposed heritage warehouses, and Ponsonby Central is a laneside collection of restaurants and cafes.

Where to Stay

Hotels dot central Auckland, while B&Bs in inner suburbs, including Ponsonby, Parnell and Mt Eden, are convenient bases for public transport and in close proximity to good eating and drinking.

Useful Websites

Tourist Information (www.aucklandnz.com) Sights, accommodation, restaurants and events.

The Denizen (www.thedenizen.co.nz) The city's best recently opened cafes, bars and restaurants.

Lonely Planet (www.lonelyplanet.com/new-zealand/auckland) Lonely Planet's city guide.

Trips Through Auckland

NEED TO KNOW

MOBILE PHONES
European phones work on New Zealand's networks; most American or Japanese phones won't. Use roaming or a local pre-paid SIM card.

INTERNET ACCESS
Wi-fi is available in most decent size towns and cities; sometimes free, sometimes hideously expensive. Internet cafes are few.

FUEL
Unleaded fuel (petrol, aka gasoline) is available from service stations across NZ, although be prepared in remote locations where there may be 100km between stations. Prices don't vary too much: per-litre costs at the time of research were around $1.80.

HIRE CARS
Ace Rental Cars (www. acerentalcars.co.nz)

Apex Car Rentals (www. apexrentals.co.nz)

Go Rentals (www.gorentals. co.nz)

IMPORTANT NUMBERS
Country code ☏ 64

Emergencies ☏ 111

Climate

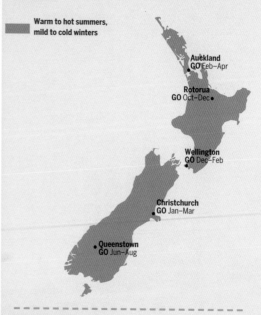

Warm to hot summers, mild to cold winters

Auckland GO Feb–Apr

Rotorua GO Oct–Dec

Wellington GO Dec–Feb

Christchurch GO Jan–Mar

Queenstown GO Jun–Aug

When to Go

High Season (Dec–Feb)
» Summer: busy beaches, outdoor explorations, festivals and sporting events.

» Big-city accommodation prices rise.

» High season in ski towns and resorts is winter (June to August).

Shoulder Season (Mar–Apr & Sep–Nov)
» Prime travelling time: fine weather, short queues, kids in school and warm(ish) ocean.

» Long evenings sipping Kiwi wines and craft beers.

Low Season (May–Aug)
» Head for the slopes of the Southern Alps for some brilliant southern-hemisphere skiing.

» Few crowds, good accommodation deals and a seat in any restaurant.

» Warm-weather beach towns may be half asleep.

Daily Costs

Budget: Less than $150

» Dorm beds or campsites: $25–38 per night

» Main course in a budget eatery: less than $15

Midrange: $150–$250

» Double room in a midrange hotel/motel: $120–200

» Main course in a midrange restaurant: $15–32

» Hire a car: from $30 per day

Top End: More than $250

» Double room in a top-end hotel: from $200

» Three-course meal in a classy restaurant: $80

» Scenic flight: from $210

Eating

Restaurants From cheap 'n' cheerful, to world-class showcasing NZ's top-notch ingredients.

Cafes Freshly roasted coffee, expert baristas, brunch-mad and family friendly.

Pubs & Bars All serve some kind of food, good and bad!

Vegetarians Well catered for, especially in cities and ethnic restaurants.

Price indicators for average cost of a main course:

$	less than $15
$$	$15–32
$$$	more than $32

Sleeping

Motels Most towns have decent, low-rise, midrange motels.

Holiday Parks Myriad options from tent sites to family units.

Hostels From party zones to family-friendly 'flashpackers'.

Hotels Range from small-town pubs to slick global-chain operations.

Price indicators for double room with bathroom in high season:

$	less than $120
$$	$120–200
$$$	more than $200

Arriving in New Zealand's North Island

Auckland International Airport

Rental Cars Major companies have desks at airport.

Buses Airbus Express buses run into the city every 10 to 30 minutes, 24 hours; door-to-door shuttles run 24 hours.

Taxis To city centre around $75 (45 minutes).

Wellington Airport

Rental Cars Major companies have desks at airport.

Buses Airport Flyer buses run to the city every 10 to 20 minutes from 6.30am to 9.30pm; door-to-door shuttles run 24 hours.

Taxis To city centre around $30 (20 minutes).

Money

ATMs are available in all cities and most towns. Credit cards are accepted almost universally, although not American Express or Diners Club.

Tipping

Optional, but 10% for great service goes down well.

Useful Websites

Lonely Planet (www.lonelyplanet.com/new-zealand) Destination information, bookings, traveller forum and more.

100% Pure New Zealand (www.newzealand.com) Official tourism site.

Department of Conservation (www.doc.govt.nz) Essential information on national parks and reserves.

Te Ara (www.teara.govt.nz) Online NZ encyclopedia.

For more, see Driving in New Zealand (p117).

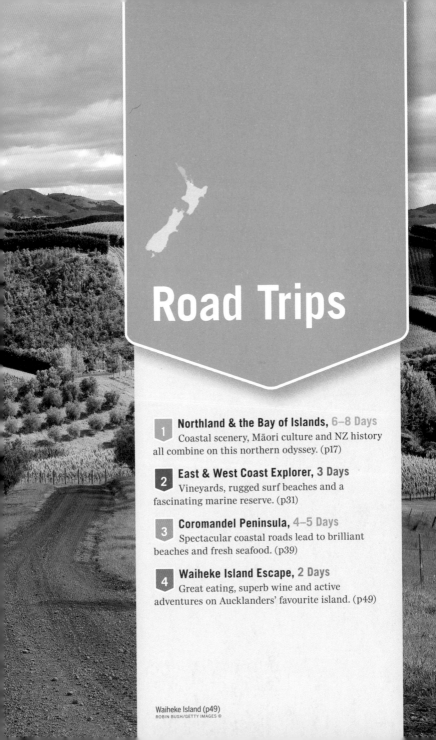

Road Trips

Waiheke Island (p49)
ROBIN BUSH/GETTY IMAGES ©

Northland & the Bay of Islands

1

Embark on this diverse northern adventure showcasing New Zealand's Māori and colonial history amid a backdrop of sparkling beaches, soaring forests and hidden harbours.

TRIP HIGHLIGHTS

559 km

Cape Reinga
Leaving point for souls to the spiritual Māori homeland

313 km

Paihia
Boat trips and the historic Waitangi Treaty Grounds

194 km

Tutukaka
Departure point for the spectacular Poor Knights Islands

787 km

Waipoua State Forest
Pay homage to giant centuries-old kauri trees

Awanui
Opononi
Hikurangi
Wellsford
START/FINISH
Auckland

**6–8 DAYS
1057KM /
658 MILES**

GREAT FOR...

BEST TIME TO GO

February to April offers the best weather, but try to avoid the busy Easter period.

ESSENTIAL PHOTO

The iconic Cape Reinga Lighthouse.

BEST FOR FAMILIES

Sandboarding down the North's giant dunes.

1

Northland & the Bay of Islands

Known as the 'Winterless North', the traditionally milder weather of this area is only one good reason to venture north of Auckland. The Bay of Islands combines Russell's heritage charm with boat cruises and marine adventures leaving from busy Paihia, and further north the attractions become even more remote and spectacular, leading all the way to the very top of the North Island at Cape Reinga.

❶ Auckland (p58)

Framed by two harbours, NZ's most cosmopolitan city spreads vibrantly across a narrow coastal isthmus. Explore Auckland's ocean-going personality at the New Zealand Maritime Museum (p81), or shoot the breeze on a sailing adventure on a genuine America's Cup yacht with **Explore** (☏0800 397 567; www.explorenz. co.nz; Viaduct Harbour). Other waterborne options include a ferry across the Waitemata harbour to the heritage Edwardian and Victorian archi-

tecture of the seaside suburb of **Devonport**, or a sea-kayaking excursion to **Rangitoto island**, a forested volcanic cone. Back on land, try our walking tour (p80), or for the best view of Rangitoto, stroll along **Takapuna Beach** on Auckland's North Shore or ride a bike around the bays along **Tamaki Drive**.

The Drive » For the first leg of 104km, depart across the Auckland Harbour Bridge heading north on SH1. North of Warkworth, turn into Wayby Valley Rd continuing on to Mangawhai Heads. Pay tolls for the Northern Gateway Toll Road on SH1 online at www.nzta. govt.nz.

❷ Mangawhai Heads (p82)

Mangawhai village lies on a horseshoe-shaped harbour, but it's Mangawhai Heads, 5km further on, that's really special. A narrow sandspit stretches for kilometres to form the harbour's south head, sheltering a **seabird sanctuary**. There's an excellent surf beach, best viewed while traversing the **Mangawhai Cliff Top Walkway**. Starting at Mangawhai Heads, this walking track (around two to three hours) offers extensive views of the ocean and the coast. Make sure you time it right to return down the beach at low tide. Other attractions around Mangawhai include **vineyards** and **olive groves**, and the **Mangawhai Museum** (☏09-431 4645; www.mangawhai-museum.org. nz; Molesworth Dr; adult/child $12/3; ⏲10am-4pm). Check out the roof shaped like a stingray. There's also a sun-drenched museum cafe here.

🔗 LINK YOUR TRIP

❷ East & West Coast Explorer

Explore to the northeast and northwest of NZ's biggest city, Auckland.

The Drive » From Mangawhai Heads continue along Cove Rd to Waipu Cove (around 13km). This is a very pretty rural and coastal route away from the busier main roads. During summer, Langs Beach en route is enlivened by the scarlet blooms of the pohutukawa, often dubbed 'NZ's Christmas tree'.

3 Waipu (p83)

The arcing beach at **Waipu Cove** looks out to Bream Bay. On the near horizon, islands include the **Hen and Chickens**. Waipu Cove is excellent for swimming – and

body surfing if there are good waves – and there are shaded spots for a picnic. A further 8km along a coastal road, Waipu is a sleepy village with excellent cafes that comes to life on summer weekends. The area was originally colonised by Scottish settlers – via Nova Scotia in Canada – who arrived between 1853 and 1860. The **Waipu Museum** (☏09-432 0746; www.waipumuseum. co.nz; 36 The Centre; adult/ child $8/3; ◷10am-4.30pm) tells their story, and on 1 January, Waipu's annual

Highland Games (www. waipugames.co.nz; adult/child $15/5) celebrate heather-infused events including caber tossing and Scottish dancing. Here's your chance to discover your inner Caledonian.

The Drive » Rejoin SH1 from Waipu via Nova Scotia Dr, and continue north to Whangarei (39km). En route, Ruakaka and Uretiti offer excellent beaches, and the imposing profile of Marsden Point announces the entrance to Whangarei Harbour.

4 Whangarei (p85)

Northland's only city has a thriving local art scene, and an attractive riverside area with excellent museums. Explore **Clapham's Clocks** (☏09-438 3993; www.claphams clocks.com; Town Basin; adult/ child $10/4; ◷9am-5pm) where more than 1400 ticking, gonging and cuckooing timepieces fill the **National Clock Museum** in Town Basin. This harbourside area is also a good place for shopping, and stores selling local arts and crafts include **Burning Issues** (☏09-438 3108; www.burningissues gallery.co.nz; Town Basin; ◷10am-5pm) and the **Bach** (☏09-438 2787; www. thebach.gallery; Town Basin; ◷9.30am-4.30pm). A 1904 Māori portrait by artist CF Goldie is a treasure of the adjacent **Whangarei Art Museum** and more contemporary art features at the **Quarry Arts**

NGĀTI TARARA

As you're travelling around the north you might notice the preponderance of road names ending in '-ich'. As the sign leading into Kaitaia proclaims, 'haere mai, dobro došli and welcome' to one of the more peculiar ethnic conjunctions in the country.

From the end of the 19th century, men from the Dalmatian coast of what is now Croatia started arriving in NZ looking for work. Many ended up in Northland's gum fields. Pākehā society wasn't particularly welcoming to the new immigrants, particularly during WWI, as they were on Austrian passports. Not so the small Māori communities of the north. Here they found an echo of Dalmatian village life, with its emphasis on extended family and hospitality, not to mention a shared history of injustice at the hands of colonial powers.

The Māori jokingly named them Tarara, as their rapid conversation in their native tongue sounded like 'ta-ra-ra-ra-ra' to Māori ears. Many Croatian men married local *wahine* (women), founding clans that have given several of today's famous Māori their Croatian surnames, like singer Margaret Urlich and former All Black Frano Botica. You'll find large Tarara communities in the Far North, Dargaville and West Auckland.

Centre (☎09-438 1215; www.quarryarts.org; 21 Selwyn Ave; ⏰9.30am-4.30pm), a raffish village of artists' studios and cooperative galleries. Around 5km west of Whangarei, **Kiwi North** (☎09-438 9630; www.kiwinorth.co.nz; 500 SH14, Maunu; adult/child $15/5; ⏰10am-4pm) combines a museum displaying Māori and colonial artefacts with a kiwi house.

The Drive 》 Depart Whangarei via Bank St, Mill St and Ngunguru Rd to Tutukaka (30km). Worthy short stops include Whangarei Falls, a spectacular 26m-high cascade 6km from Town Basin, and Ngunguru, a sleepy estuary settlement just before Tutukaka.

`TRIP HIGHLIGHT`

❺ Tutukaka (p88)

Bursting with yachts, dive crews and game-fishing charter boats, the **marina** at Tutukaka presents opportunities to explore the stunning above- and below-water scenery in the surrounding area. Many travellers are here to go diving at the **Poor Knights Islands**, but the underwater thrills are also accessible for snorkelling fans. Surfing lessons are available from **O'Neill Surf Academy** (☎09-434 3843; www.oneillsurfacademy.co.nz; 66 Te Maika Rd, Ngunguru; 2hr lesson from $75, one-day option $125), and one of the best local walks is a blissful

MARINE RICHES AT THE POOR KNIGHTS

Established in 1981, the Poor Knights marine reserve is rated as one of the world's top-10 diving spots. The islands are bathed in a subtropical current from the Coral Sea, so varieties of tropical and subtropical fish not seen in other NZ waters can be observed here. The waters are clear, with no sediment or pollution problems. The 40m to 60m underwater cliffs drop steeply to the sandy bottom and are a labyrinth of archways, caves, tunnels and fissures that attract a wide variety of sponges and colourful underwater vegetation. Schooling fish, eels and rays are common (including manta rays in season).

The two main volcanic islands, **Tawhiti Rahi** and **Aorangi**, were home to the Ngāi Wai tribe, but since a raiding-party massacre by the Te Hikutu tribe in 1825, the islands have been *tapu* (forbidden). Even today the public is barred from the islands, in order to protect their pristine environment. Not only do tuatara (reptile) and Butler's shearwater (pelagic seabird) breed here, but there are unique species of flora, such as the Poor Knights lily.

To explore the Poor Knights underwater, contact **Dive! Tutukaka** (p88). For nondivers, it also offers the **Perfect Day Ocean Cruise** including snorkelling, kayaking, paddle boarding, and sightings of dolphins (usually) and whales (occasionally). Cruises run from November to May.

20-minute coastal stroll from **Matapouri** to the compact cove at nearby **Whale Bay**.

The Drive 》 Allow two hours for this 106km leg. Leaving Tutukaka and heading north, the coastal road veers inland before reaching the coast again at Matapouri. From Matapouri, continue west to SH1 at Hikurangi. Head north on SH1, and turn right into Russell Rd just before Whakapara. Featuring coastal scenery, this winding road – take care – continues via Helena Bay to Russell.

---

❻ Russell (p89)

Once known as 'the hellhole of the Pacific', Russell is a historic town with cafes and genteel B&Bs. Russell was originally Kororareka, a fortified Ngāpuhi village. In the early 19th century the local Māori tribe permitted it to become NZ's first European settlement. It quickly attracted roughnecks like fleeing convicts, whalers and drunken sailors, and

WHIT PRESTON/GETTY IMAGES ©

SCOTT ESPIE/GETTY IMAGES ©

WHY THIS IS A CLASSIC TRIP
BRETT ATKINSON, WRITER

The oft-present coastline is this journey's defining feature. Secondary highways off busy SH1 combine for ongoing glimpses of beautiful bays and coves, often negotiating winding routes to showcase sleepy anchorages like the Whangaroa or Hokianga Harbours. All the while, the intersecting stories of Māori and colonial settlers conspire to provide a fascinating heritage counterpoint essential to understanding NZ history.

Top: Hiking in Waipu (p20)
Left: Rock pools, Tutukaka (p21)
Right: Māori meeting house, Waitangi Treaty Grounds, Paihia

in 1835 Charles Darwin described it as full of 'the refuse of society'. After the signing of the Treaty of Waitangi in 1840, nearby Okiato was the country's temporary capital before the capital was moved to Auckland in 1841. Okiato, then known as Russell, was abandoned, and the name Russell eventually replaced Kororareka. Historical highlights now include **Pompallier Mission**, an 1842 Catholic mission house, and **Christ Church** (1836), NZ's oldest church.

The Drive ⟩⟩ It's about 8km to Okiato. A car ferry (car/motorcycle/passenger $11/5.50/1) – cash payment only and buy tickets on board – crosses regularly from Okiato to Opua (5km from Paihia).

TRIP HIGHLIGHT

❼ Paihia (p91)

Connected to Russell by passenger ferries across a narrow harbour, Paihia is more energetic than its sleepier sibling. Motels and backpacker hostels are crammed during summer holidays, and Paihia's waterfront hosts maritime excursions including island sightseeing, dolphin-watching and sailing. A coastal road meanders 3km to the **Waitangi Treaty Grounds**. Occupying a headland draped in lawns and forest, this is NZ's most important historic site. On 6 February 1840, the first 43 of more than 500 Māori chiefs signed the Treaty of Waitangi with the British Crown. Admission to the Treaty Grounds includes guided tours, Māori cultural performances and entry to the **Museum of Waitangi** (p91), a showcase of the treaty in NZ's past, present and future.

The Drive » From Paihia, continue on SH11 (Black Bridge Rd) to Kerikeri, a meandering 24km route through citrus orchards. Around 4km from Paihia, the spectacular Haruru Falls can be reached by turning off Puketona Rd onto Haruru Falls Rd.

----

8 Kerikeri (p95)

Famous for its oranges, Kerikeri also produces kiwifruit, vegetables and wine. It's also increasingly popular with retirees and hosts some of the Northland's best restaurants. A snapshot of early Māori and Pākehā (European New Zealander) interaction is offered by a cluster of historic sites centred on Kerikeri's picturesque river basin. Dating from 1836, the **Stone Store** ([phone]09-407 9236; www.historic.org.nz; 246 Kerikeri Rd; ⏰10am-4pm) is NZ's oldest stone building, and tours depart from here for the nearby **Mission House** (www.historic.org.nz; tours $10), NZ's oldest surviving building, dating from 1822. There's an ongoing campaign to have the area recognised as a Unesco World Heritage site.

The Drive » From Kerikeri, head north on SH10, turning east to Matauri Bay Rd to complete a stunning 41km loop back to SH10 just north of Kaeo. This coastal road takes in Matauri Bay, Tauranga Bay and the expansive Whangaroa Harbour. Back on SH10, continue 30km north to Mangonui, 90km from Kerikeri, and Doubtless Bay.

----

9 Mangonui (p98)

Doubtless Bay gets its name from an entry in Captain James Cook's logbook, where he wrote that the body of water was 'doubtless a bay'. The main centre, Mangonui ('Big Shark'), retains a fishing-port ambience, and cafes and galleries fill its historic waterfront buildings. They were constructed when Mangonui was a centre of the whaling industry

DETOUR: KAWAKAWA

Start: 7 Paihia

Located 17km south of Paihia on SH11, Kawakawa is just an ordinary Kiwi town, but the public toilets (60 Gillies St) are anything but. They were designed by Austrian-born artist and eco-architect Friedensreich Hundertwasser, who lived near Kawakawa in an isolated house without electricity from 1973 until his death in 2000. The most photographed toilets in NZ are typical Hundertwasser – lots of organic wavy lines decorated with ceramic mosaics and brightly coloured bottles, and with grass and plants on the roof. Other examples of his work can be seen in Vienna and Osaka.

Kawakawa also has a railway line running down the main street. Take a 45-minute spin pulled by **Gabriel the Steam Engine** ([phone]09-404 0684; www.bayofislandsvintagerailway.org.nz; adult/child $20/5; ⏰10.45am, noon, 1.15pm & 2.30pm Fri-Sun, daily school holidays). South of town, a signpost from SH1 points to **Kawiti Glowworm Caves** ([phone]09-404 0583; www.kawiticaves.co.nz; 49 Waiomio Rd; adult/child $20/10; ⏰8.30am-4.30pm) – around 5km. Explore the insect-illuminated caverns with a 30-minute subterranean tour. Guided tours only.

If you're travelling from Okiato to Opua on the car ferry, Kawakawa is 12km south of the Opua ferry landing on SH11.

LOCAL KNOWLEDGE: KERIKERI COTTAGE INDUSTRIES

You'd be forgiven for thinking that everyone in Kerikeri is involved in some small-scale artisanal enterprise, as the bombardment of craft shops on the way into town attests.

While Northland isn't known for its wine, a handful of vineyards are doing their best to change that. The little-known red grape chambourcin has proved particularly suited to the region's subtropical humidity, along with pinotage and syrah.

Look out for the *Art & Craft Trail* and *Wine Trail* brochures. Here are our tasty recommendations.

Kerikeri Farmers Market (www.boifm.org.nz; Hobson Ave; ⊙8.30am-noon Sun) From gourmet sausages to limoncello.

Old Packhouse Market (☎09-401 9588; www.theoldpackhousemarket.co.nz; 505 Kerikeri Rd; ⊙8am-1.30pm Sat) Combines a farmers market with great breakfasts.

Get Fudged & Keriblue Ceramics (☎09-407 1111; www.keriblueceramics.co.nz; 560 Kerikeri Rd; ⊙9am-5pm) An unusual pairing of ceramics and big, decadent slabs of fudge.

Makana Confections (☎09-407 6800; www.makana.co.nz; 504 Kerikeri Rd; ⊙9am-5.30pm) Artisanal chocolate factory with lots of sampling.

Marsden Estate (☎09-407 9398; www.marsdenestate.co.nz; 56 Wiroa Rd; ⊙10am-5pm) Excellent wine and lunch on the deck.

Ake Ake (☎09-407 8230; www.akeakevineyard.co.nz; 165 Waimate North Rd; tastings $5; ⊙cellar door 10am-4.30pm, restaurant noon-3pm & 6-9pm Mon-Sat, noon-3pm Sun, reduced hours outside summer) Wine tastings are free with lunch or purchase of wine, and the restaurant is one of Northland's best.

Cottle Hill (☎09-407 5203; www.cottlehill.co.nz; Cottle Hill Dr; tastings $5, free with purchase; ⊙10am-5.30pm Nov-Mar, 10am-5pm Wed-Sun Apr-Oct) Wine and port.

Byrne Northland Wines (Fat Pig Wine Cellar; ☎09-407 3113; www.byrnewine.com/wordpress; 177 Puketotara Rd; ⊙11am-7pm) Excellent viognier and rosé.

(1792–1850) and exported flax, kauri timber and gum. At Hihi, 15km northeast of Mangonui, the **Butler Point Whaling Museum** (☎0800 687 386; www.butlerpoint.co.nz; Marchant Rd, Hihi; adult/child $20/5; ⊙by appointment) showcases these earlier days. The nearby settlements of Coopers Beach, Cable Bay and Taipa are all pockets of beachside gentrification and well-tanned retirees with golf habits.

The Drive » This leg is 132km. From Mangonui, drive west on SH10 to rejoin SH1 at Awanui. From Awanui head to NZ's northernmost point, Cape Reinga. An interesting stop is at the Nga-Tapuwae-o-te-Mangai Māori Ratana temple at Te Kao, 58km north of Awanui. Look out for the two green-and-white domed towers.

TRIP HIGHLIGHT

⑩ Cape Reinga (p99)

The water off the windswept **Cape Reinga Lighthouse** (a rolling 1km walk from the car park) is where the Tasman Sea and Pacific Ocean meet, crashing into waves up to 10m high in stormy weather.

Māori consider Cape Reinga (Te Rerenga-Wairua) the jumping-off point for souls as they depart on the journey to their spiritual homeland. Out of respect to the most sacred site of Māori people, refrain from eating or drinking anywhere in the area. Around 16km south of Cape Reinga on SH1, a road leads west for 4km to the **Te Paki Recreation Reserve** (p99). During summer, **Ahikaa Adventures** (p100) rents sandboards to toboggan down the reserve's giant dunes.

The Drive ›› It is possible to drive down Ninety Mile Beach, but every year several tourists – and their rental cars – get hopelessly stuck in the sand. Either join a 4WD bus tour or drive south to Kaitaia from Cape Reinga on SH1 (111km) and continue 13km west to Ahipara on the Ahipara Rd.

- - - - - - - - - - - -

⑪ Ahipara (p100)

All good things must come to an end, and Ninety Mile Beach does at this relaxed Far North beach town. A few holiday mansions have snuck in, but mostly it's just the locals keeping it real with visiting surfers. The area is known for its huge sand dunes and massive gum field where 2000 people once worked. Adventure activities are popular on the dunes above Ahipara

and further around the Tauroa Peninsula. **Ahipara Adventure Centre** (p101) can hook you up with sand toboggans, surfboards, mountain bikes, blokarts for sand yachting and quad-bikes, and Ahipara-based **NZ Surf Bros** (p101) offers surfing lessons.

The Drive ›› From Ahipara, drive 64km through the verdant Herekino forest to the sleepy harbour settlement of Kohukohu. Around 4km past Kohukohu, a car ferry (car/ campervan/motorcycle/ passenger $20/40/5/2) crosses the Hokianga Harbour to Rawene. Payment is cash only and the ferry leaves Kohukohu on the hour from 8am to 8pm.

- - - - - - - - - - - -

⑫ Rawene (p101)

During the height of the kauri industry Kohukohu was a busy town with a sawmill, shipyard, two newspapers and banks. These days it's a very quiet harbour backwater dotted with well-preserved heritage buildings. Have a coffee and one of NZ's best pies at the local cafe, before catching the ferry across the harbour to Rawene. Founded as NZ's third European settlement, a number of historic buildings (including six churches) remain from a time when the harbour was considerably busier than it is now. Information boards outline a

heritage trail of the main sights. Built in the bustling 1860s by a trader, stately **Clendon House** (p101) is now managed by the New Zealand Historic Places Trust. A few browse-worthy **art galleries** fill other historic buildings.

The Drive ›› After crossing on the vehicle ferry from Kohukohu to Rawene, another winding road and scenic road travels 20km to reach Opononi, near the entrance of Hokianga Harbour.

- - - - - - - - - - - -

⑬ Opononi & Omapere (p102)

The twin settlements of Opononi and Omapere lie on the south head of Hokianga Harbour. Views are dominated by mountainous sand dunes across the water at North Head. During summer, the **Hokianga Express** (📱021 405 872, 09-405 8872; per tour $27; ⏰10am-2pm summer) departs from Opononi Jetty, and travellers can sandboard down a 30m slope. Body boards are provided and bookings are essential. Starting at the car park at the end of Signal Station Rd – right off SH12 at the top of the hill leaving **Omapere** – the **Arai te Uru Heritage Walk** (30 minutes return) follows the cliffs and passes through manuka scrub before continuing to the

---

Right Rawene

TOM ANG/GETTY IMAGES ©

Hokianga's southern headland. At the headland are the remains of an old **signal station** built to assist ships making the treacherous passage into the harbour.

The Drive » Climbing south out of Omapere – don't miss the spectacular views back across the harbour – SH12 continues to the Waipoua Forest – a meandering journey of around 20km.

TRIP HIGHLIGHT

⑭ Waipoua Forest (p103)

This superb forest sanctuary – proclaimed in 1952 after public pressure – is the largest remnant of the once-extensive kauri forests of northern NZ. The forest road (SH12) stretches for 18km and passes huge trees. Near the northern end of the park stands mighty **Tane Mahuta**, named for the Māori forest god. At 51.5m high with a 13.8m girth, this is the largest kauri alive, and has been growing for between 1200 and 2000 years. Stop at the **Waipoua Forest Visitor Centre** (☎09-439 6445; www.teroroa.iwi.nz/visit-waipoua; 1 Waipoua River Rd; ◷9am-6.30pm summer, 9am-4pm winter) for an exhibition on the forests, guided tours, flax-weaving lessons and a cafe. You can also plant your own kauri tree, complete with GPS co-ordinates. Other massive trees to discover include

DETOUR: KARIKARI PENINSULA

Start: ⑨ **Mangonui**

Around 9km west of Taipa on SH10, head north on Inland Rd to explore the Karikari Peninsula, The oddly shaped peninsula bends into a near-perfect right angle. The result is beaches facing north, south, east and west in close proximity. This unique set-up makes Karikari Peninsula one of the world's best spots for kiteboarding, or at least that's the opinion of the experienced crew at **Airzone Kitesurfing School** (☎021 202 7949; www.kitesurfnz.com; 1-/2-/3-day course $195/350/485). Learners get to hone their skills on flat water before heading to the surf.

Despite its natural assets, the peninsula is blissfully undeveloped, with farmers well outnumbering tourist operators. Sun-kissed highlights include **Tokerau Beach**, a long, sandy stretch on the western edge of Doubtless Bay. Neighbouring **Whatuwhiwhi** is smaller and more built-up, facing back across the bay. **Maitai Bay**, with its tiny twin coves, is the loveliest of them all, at the lonely end of the peninsula down an unsealed road. It's a great sheltered spot for swimming. **Rangiputa** faces west at the elbow of the peninsula; the pure white sand and crystal-clear sheltered waters come straight from a Pacific Island daydream. A turn-off on the road to Rangiputa takes you to remote **Puheke Beach**, a long, windswept stretch of snow-white sand dunes forming Karikari's northern edge.

Eating opportunities are limited so stock up for a beachside picnic in Mangonui, or stop in at **Karikari Estate** (☎09-408 7222; www.karikariestate.co.nz; Maitai Bay Rd; tastings $15; ◷11am-4pm Oct-Apr, pizza evenings from 5pm late Dec-Feb). This impressive vineyard produces acclaimed red wines and has a cafe attached (mains and platters $16 to $40). During the peak of summer, good pizza is served in the cafe. Count on 80km for a return trip from Mangonui to the Karikari Peninsula.

Te Matua Ngahere (p103) and the **Four Sisters**.

The Drive » From the Waipoua Forest Visitor Centre, it's 107km on SH12 – via the riverine town of Dargaville – to Matakohe. Around 4km north of Dargaville, Baylys Coast Rd runs 9km west to Baylys Beach, a wild surf beach.

- - - - - - - - - - -

⑮ Matakohe (p104)

Apart from the rural charms of this village, the key reason for visiting Matakohe is the superb **Kauri Museum** (☏09-431 7417; www.kauri museum.com; 5 Church Rd; adult/child $25/8; ⊙9am-5pm). The giant cross-sections of trees are astounding, but the entire timber industry is brought to life through video kiosks, artefacts, fabulous furniture and marquetry, and reproductions of a pioneer sawmill, boarding house, gumdigger's hut and Victorian home. The Gum Room holds a weird and wonderful collection of kauri gum, the amber substance that can be carved, sculpted and polished to a jewel-like quality. The museum shop stocks mementos crafted from kauri wood and gum.

LOCAL KNOWLEDGE: EXPLORING THE FOREST AFTER DARK

Led by Māori guides, this four-hour twilight tour into Waipoua Forest by **Footprints Waipoua** (☏09-405 8207; www.footprintswaipoua.co.nz; adult/child $95/35; ⊙from 5pm Apr-Oct, 6pm Nov-Mar) is a fantastic introduction to both the culture and the forest giants. Tribal history and stories are shared, and mesmerising *karakia* (prayer, incantation) recited before the gargantuan trees. Daytime tours ($80) are also available, but the twilight tours amplify the sense of spirituality. Tours depart from the Copthorne Hotel & Resort on SH12 in Omapere.

The Drive » From Matakohe, travel east on SH12 to join SH1 again at Brynderwyn. Drive south to Wellsford and then take SH16 for the scenic route southwest back to Auckland (163km in total from Matakohe). From Wellsford to Auckland on SH16 is around 110km, taking in views of Kaipara Harbour and West Auckland's vineyards.

East & West Coast Explorer

2

From Auckland, embark on a circular route north of the city to uncover secluded and spectacular beaches, sophisticated vineyard restaurants and a menu of family-friendly activities.

TRIP HIGHLIGHTS

81 km

Goat Island
A marine reserve packed with underwater life

4

● Wellsford

3

Warkworth ●

66 km

Matakana
Vineyards, a farmers market and a local arts scene

● Helensville

● Kumeu

START/ FINISH
● Auckland

6

9

Muriwai
Gannets nest above this sprawling black sand surf beach

Piha
Lion Rock stands sentinel at this West Coast beach

200 km

275 km

---

3 DAYS
317KM / 197 MILES

GREAT FOR...

BEST TIME TO GO

February to April for leisurely vineyard lunches.

ESSENTIAL PHOTO

Piha's Lion Rock from high above the beach.

BEST FOR FAMILIES

Viewing the underwater spectacle at Goat Island.

2 East & West Coast Explorer

The proud residents of Auckland are a lucky bunch, and this trip takes in some of their favourite day-escapes from the energy and bustle of the city. Plan your route to be slightly more leisurely, and enjoy a few days blending virtue and vice by combining fine wine, beer and local markets with coastal bush walks, beaches and active adventure.

---

1 Auckland (p58)

Before heading off on a journey where food, wine and markets are tasty features, explore the culinary scene of New Zealand's most diverse and cosmopolitan city. The best farmers market is at **La Cigale** (☎09-366 9361; www.lacigale.co.nz; 69 St Georges Bay Rd, Parnell; cafe $8-18, bistro $12-22; ⊙market 9am-1.30pm Sat & Sun, cafe 9am-4pm Mon-Fri, to 2pm Sat & Sun, bistro 6pm-late Wed-Fri), where stalls are laden with local goodies on Saturday and Sunday morning. Many of the stalls are run by recent arrivals contributing to Auckland's irresistible ethnic collage. On Wednesday evenings La Cigale

becomes a food-truck stop, while on Thursdays and Fridays the space is converted into a quirky evening bistro serving simple rustic dishes. For a small-group city tour, including market visits, craft beer pubs, artisan producers and loads of tastings, hook up with the crew at **Big Foody** (☎021 481 177, 0800 366 386; www.thebigfoody.com; per person $125-185), or take our walking tour (p80).

The Drive » Head north on SH1 and turn left to Puhoi after the spectacular Johnstone Hills tunnels. Pay tolls ($2.30) for the Northern Gateway Toll Road on SH1 online at www.nzta.govt.nz. The total distance of this leg is 43km.

Port Albert

Kaipara Harbour

16

Parakai

5 **Helensvill**

Woodhill Forest

Woodhill

Waimauku

6 **Muriwai**

8 **Te Henga (Bethells Beach)**

TASMAN SEA

9 **Piha**

Karekare

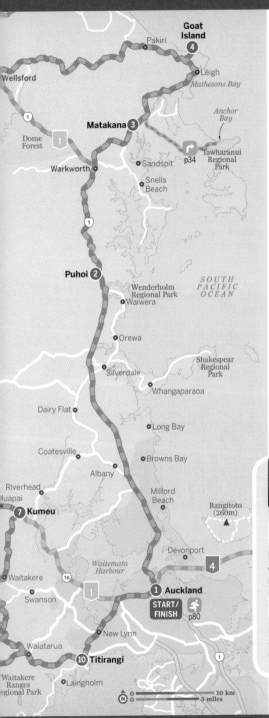

2 Puhoi (p71)

Forget dingy cafes and earnest poets – this quaint riverside village is a slice of the real Bohemia. In 1863, around 200 German-speaking immigrants from the present-day Czech Republic settled in what was then dense bush. The **Bohemian Museum** (☎09-422 0852; www.puhoihistoricalsociety.org.nz; Puhoi Rd; adult/child $3.50/free; ☉noon-3pm Sat & Sun, daily Jan-Easter) tells the story of the hardship and perseverance of these original pioneers. Raise a glass to their endeavour and endurance at the character-filled **Puhoi Pub** (p72). **Puhoi River Canoe Hire** (☎09-422 0891; www.puhoirivercanoes.co.nz; 84 Puhoi Rd) rents kayaks and Canadian canoes, either by the hour (kayak/canoe $25/50), or for an excellent 8km downstream

LINK YOUR TRIP

1 Northland & the Bay of Islands

New Zealand's Māori and colonial history unfold to the north along both coasts.

4 Waiheke Island Escape

Use Auckland as a base for more stellar beaches and vineyard restaurants.

journey from the village to Wenderholm Regional Park (single/double kayak $50/100, including return transport). Bookings are essential.

The Drive » Continue north on SH1 and turn right just after Warkworth to negotiate wine country and pretty coastal coves to Matakana, 25km from Puhoi.

---

❸ Matakana (p72)

Around 15 years ago, Matakana was a rural village with a handful of heritage buildings and an old-fashioned country pub. Now its stylish wine bars and cafes are a weekend destination for day-tripping Aucklanders. An excellent Saturday morning **farmers market** (www. matakanavillage.co.nz; Mata-kana Sq, 2 Matakana Valley Rd; ⏰8am-1pm Sat) is held in a shaded riverside location, and the area's boutique wineries are becoming renowned for pinot gris, merlot, syrah and a host of obscure varietals. Local vineyards are detailed in the free *Matakana Coast Wine Country* (www.matakanacoast .com) and *Matakana Wine Trail* (www. matakanawine.com) brochures, available from the **Matakana information centre** (☎09-422 7433; www.matakanainfo.org.nz; 2 Matakana Valley Rd; ⏰10am-1pm). A local arts scene is anchored by **Morris & James** (☎09-422 7116; www. morrisandjames.co.nz; 48 Tongue Farm Rd; ⏰9am-5pm), a well-established potters' workshop.

The Drive » Leave Matakana on Leigh Rd and continue through the seaside village of Leigh before turning right into Goat Island Rd. Twelve kilometres north of Matakana, Mathesons Bay is a secluded cove with good swimming. The total distance to Goat Island is 16km.

---

❹ Goat Island (p72)

This 547-hectare aquatic area was established in 1975 as the country's first **marine reserve** (www.doc. govt.nz; Goat Island Rd), and has now developed into a giant outdoor aquarium. Wade knee-deep into the water to see snapper (the big fish with blue dots and fins), blue maomao and stripy parore swimming around. Excellent interpretive panels explain the area's Māori significance (it was the landing place of one of the ancestral canoes) and provide pictures of the species you're likely to encounter. Hire snorkels and wetsuits from **Goat Island Dive & Snorkel** (p73) in Leigh or join a 45-minute boat trip with **Glass Bottom Boat Tours** (p73).

The Drive » Continue to Wellsford (34km) before taking SH16 to meander another 57km southwest through farmland and past Kaipara Harbour to Helensville.

DETOUR: TAWHARANUI REGIONAL PARK

Start: ❸ Matakana

Around 1.5km northeast of Matakana en route to Leigh and Goat Island, turn right on Takatu Rd to follow a partly unsealed route for around 14km to **Tawharanui Regional Park** (☎09-366 2000; http:// regionalparks.aucklandcouncil.govt.nz/tawharanui; 1181 Takatu Rd), a 588-hectare reserve at the end of a peninsula. This special place is an open sanctuary for native birds, protected by a pest-proof fence, while the northern coast is a marine park (bring a snorkel). There are plenty of **walking tracks** (1½ to four hours) but the main attraction is **Anchor Bay**, one of the region's finest white-sand beaches.

Camping is allowed at two basic sites near the beach (adult/child $15/6) and there's a six-person bach for hire ($168).

⑤ Helensville (p71)

Heritage buildings, antique shops and cafes make village-like Helensville a good whistle-stop for those negotiating SH16. Energetic and relaxing activities also combine for an interesting destination that's perfect for adventurous families. At the **Woodhill Mountain Bike Park** (📞027 278 0969; www.bikepark.co.nz; Restall Rd, Woodhill; adult/child $8/6, bike hire from $30; ⏰8am-5.30pm Thu-Tue, 8am-10pm Wed) 14km south of Helensville, challenging tracks (including jumps and beams) career through the Woodhill Forest, and at **Tree Adventures** (📞0800 827 926; www.treeadventures.co.nz; Restall Rd, Woodhill; ropes courses $17-42; ⏰10am-5pm Sat & Sun) high-ropes courses include swinging logs, climbing nets and a flying fox. Nearby **Parakai Springs** (📞09-420 8998; www.parakaisprings.co.nz; 150 Parkhurst Rd; adult/child $22/11; ⏰10am-9pm) has thermally heated swimming pools, private spas and a couple of hydroslides.

The Drive » Continue south on SH16 to Waimauku (17km) and turn right for the 8km to Muriwai. Look forward to rolling pastures dotted with sheep, followed by a winding drive through the forest.

LOCAL KNOWLEDGE: THE WILD WEST COAST

Peter Hillary, Mountaineer & Explorer
My family grew up loving Auckland's wild west coast, where the Tasman Sea pounds the black-sand beaches and black-back gulls ride the westerlies. Our family has walked and explored and lived out here for nearly a century and this is also where we came to grieve after my mother and sister were killed in 1975, where the invigorating salty air and the marvellous wild vistas to the Tasman Sea worked like a balm for our broken hearts. My father [Sir Edmund Hillary] would come here to dream up and then prepare for new expeditionary challenges. It seemed the right sort of environment for someone like him: not a passive coastline, but active and exciting, with huge cliffs, crashing waves, thick bush and a tantalising far-away horizon.

TRIP HIGHLIGHT

⑥ Muriwai

A black-sand surf beach, Muriwai features the **Takapu Refuge gannet colony**, which is spread over the southern headland and outlying rock stacks. Viewing platforms get you close enough to watch (and smell) these fascinating seabirds. Every August hundreds of adult birds return to this spot to hook up with their regular partners and get busy in spectacular (and noisy) displays of courting. The net result is a single chick per season; December and January are the best times to see them testing their wings before embarking on an impressive odyssey to Australia. Nearby, two short tracks wind through beautiful native bush to a **lookout** that offers views along the 60km length of the beach. Note this wild beach is only safe for swimming when patrolled. Always swim between the flags.

The Drive » Return to SH16 and turn right to Kumeu. Orchards and vineyards feature along this 16km route, and it's a good area to buy fresh fruit.

---

⑦ Kumeu (p70)

West Auckland's main wine-producing area still has some vineyards owned by the original Croatian families who kick-started NZ's wine industry. The fancy eateries that have mushroomed in recent years have done little to dint the relaxed farmland feel to the region, but everything to encourage an afternoon's indulgence on the way back from the beach or the hot pools. Most cellars offer free tastings. Top vineyards include **Coopers Creek** (p70), **Kumeu River** (p70) and **Soljans Estate** (🕿 09-412 5858; www.soljans.co.nz; 366 SH16; ⏱ tastings 9am-5pm, cafe 10am-3pm). **Hallertau** (p71), at nearby **Riverhead**, is an excellent craft brewery also with very good food.

The Drive » Depart Kumeu on Waitakere Rd and turn right into Bethells Rd after 10km. It's 12km further to Te Henga (Bethells Beach).

- - - - - - - - - -

8 Te Henga (Bethells Beach; p70)

Breathtaking Bethells Beach is a raw, black-sand beach with surf, windswept dunes and walks, such as the popular one over giant sand dunes to **Lake Wainamu** (starting near the bridge on the approach to the beach). If you're keen to stay the night at this rugged and beautiful spot, enquire about glamping at Bethells Cafe.

The Drive » Leave Bethells Beach on Bethells Rd which veers into Te Henga Rd. Around 11km from Bethells Beach turn right into Scenic Dr and follow this winding bush-clad route before turning back towards the

SUNREAL/SHUTTERSTOCK ©

coast onto Piha Rd. This leg is 37km in total.

- - - - - - - - - -

TRIP HIGHLIGHT

9 Piha (p68)

This beautifully rugged, black-sand beach has long been a favourite for Aucklanders for day trips, teenage weekend roadies, or family holidays. Although Piha is popular, it's also incredibly dangerous with wild surf and strong undercurrents. Always swim between the flags, where lifeguards can see if you get into trouble. Near the centre of the beach is **Lion Rock** (101m), whose 'mane' glows golden in the evening light. It's actually the eroded core of an ancient volcano and a Māori *pa* (fortified village) site. A path at the southern end of the beach leads to great lookouts. At low tide you can walk south along the beach and watch the surf shooting through a ravine in another large rock known as **The Camel**.

The Drive » Piha Rd leads back into Scenic Dr, which continues through West Auckland suburbs to Titirangi, 25km from Piha.

Piha and Lion Rock

⑩ Titirangi

This little village marks the end of Auckland's suburban sprawl and is a good place to spot all manner of Westie stereotypes over a coffee, wine or cold beer. Once home to NZ's greatest modern painter, Colin McCahon, there remains an artsy feel to the place. It's a mark of the esteem in which McCahon is held that the house he lived and painted in during the 1950s has been opened to the public as a mini-museum (☎09-817 7200; www. mccahonhouse.org.nz; 67 Otitori Bay Rd, French Bay; admission $5; ◷1-4pm Wed-Sun) . The swish pad next door is temporary home to the artist lucky enough to win the McCahon Arts Residence. Look for the signposts pointing down Park Rd, just before you reach Titirangi village. More art is on display at the **Te Uru Waitakere Contemporary Gallery** (☎09-817 8087; www.teuru. org.nz; 420 Titirangi Rd; admission free; ◷10am-4.30pm), an excellent modern gallery housed in the former Hotel Titirangi (1930) on the edge of the village. Titirangi means 'Fringe of Heaven' – an apt name given its proximity to the verdant Waitakere Ranges.

The Drive » From Titirangi, continue through the west Auckland suburbs of New Lynn and Avondale to rejoin the motorway (SH16) back to central Auckland, 17km from Titirangi, at Waterview.

Coromandel Peninsula

3

Meandering coastal roads weave a magical path on this journey around the compact but colourful Coromandel Peninsula. Visit in January for the crimson splash of pohutukawa blossoms.

TRIP HIGHLIGHTS

63 km
Coromandel Town
Ride a quirky railway and feast on seafood
● Colville

186 km
Hahei
Spend a leisurely few hours in beautiful Cathedral Cove

③

● Whitianga

⑦

⑧

194 km
Hot Water Beach
Dig yourself a natural sandy spa pool

● Thames
START

● Whangamata

288 km
Waihi
Explore the area's fascinating history of gold-mining

⑩
● Waihi Beach
FINISH

4–5 DAYS
299KM /
186 MILES

GREAT FOR...

BEST TIME TO GO
November to April, but try to avoid school holidays, Christmas and Easter.

 ESSENTIAL PHOTO

The graceful and spectacular arch of Cathedral Cove.

 BEST FOR BEACHES

The beautiful sandy arc of Opito.

3 Coromandel Peninsula

A favourite holiday spot for residents of nearby Auckland and Hamilton, the Coromandel Peninsula packs attractions aplenty into its beach-fringed coastline. The legacy of a gold-mining past lingers in the heritage streets of Thames, Coromandel Town and Waihi, and natural attractions like Cathedral Cove and Hot Water Beach combine with exciting and diverse opportunities to explore and get active around a stunning marine-scape.

① Thames (p105)

Heritage wooden buildings from the 19th-century gold rush still dominate Thames – especially in the stately shopfronts along Pollen St – but grizzly prospectors have long been replaced by laid-back locals. Learn about the area's gold-flecked history at the **Goldmine Experience** – including watching a giant stamper battery effortlessly crush rock – and at the interesting **School of Mines & Mineralogical Museum**. The weekly **Thames Market** (⏍07-868 9841; Pollen St, Grahamstown; ⏣8am-noon

Sat) is packed with local arts and crafts, and Thames is also a good base for tramping or canyoning in the nearby **Kauaeranga Valley**.

The Drive » Heading north up the Coromandel Peninsula's west coast, narrow SH25 meanders past pretty bays. At Tapu, 20km north of Thames, turn inland for 6km on a mainly sealed road to the Rapaura Water Gardens.

② Rapaura Water Gardens

Beautifully located in a verdant stand of native forest, the **Rapaura Water Gardens** (⏍07-868 4821; www.rapaurawatergardens.co.nz;

586 Tapu-Coroglen Rd; adult/child $15/6; ⏱9am-5pm) are a relaxing combination of water, greenery and art. Lily ponds, compact bridges and sculptures crafted from punga (a fern native to New Zealand) all blend at this soothing diversion from SH25, and there's also a very good cafe here (mains $14 to $29) and on-site accommodation (cottage/lodge $165/285).

The Drive » Rejoin SH25 at Tapu and continue north for 35km to Coromandel Town. Look forward to stunning coastal views, especially as you drop down off the winding hill road for the final drive into town.

`TRIP HIGHLIGHT`

❸ Coromandel Town (p107)

Crammed with heritage buildings, Coromandel Town is a thoroughly quaint little place. Its natty cafes, interesting art stores, excellent sleeping options and delicious smoked mussels could keep you here longer than you expected. The **Driving Creek Railway & Potteries** (☏07-866 8703; www.drivingcreekrailway.co.nz; 380 Driving Creek Rd; adult/child $35/13; ⏱10.15am & 2pm, additional times in summer) was a lifelong labour of love for its conservationist owner, well-known potter, the late Barry Brickell. This unique train runs up

LAURIE NOBLE/GETTY IMAGES ©

steep grades, across four trestle bridges, along two spirals and a double switchback, and through two tunnels, finishing at the 'Eye-full Tower'. The one-hour trip passes artworks and regenerating native forest – more than 17,000 natives have been planted, including 9000 kauri trees. Booking ahead is recommended in summer.

**The Drive ›› **Leave Coromandel Town on Kapanga Rd, the settlement's sleepy main drag. Kapanga Rd leads into Rings Rd and then into Colville Rd. From Coromandel Town to Colville is around 27km, a stunning route negotiating beautiful beaches including Oamaru Bay and Amodeo Bay.

- - - - - - - - - - - - - - -

④ Colville (p109)

The tiny settlement of Colville is a remote rural community fringed by a muddy bay and framed by rolling green pastures. If you're continuing on the unsealed roads of Far North Coromandel, the **Colville General Store** (p109) is your last stop for both petrol and organic food. Wise travellers should plan ahead for both. Around 1km south of Colville, the **Mahamudra Centre** (☎07-866 6851; www. mahamudra.org.nz; RD4, Main Rd, Colville; campsite/dm/s/tw $18/28/50/80) is a serene Tibetan Buddhist retreat with a stupa, meditation hall and regular meditation courses. It offers

simple accommodation in a park-like setting. Visiting is not possible if a retreat is scheduled, so phone ahead to check.

**The Drive ›› **Return south from Colville and turn east onto SH25 around 500m south of Coromandel Town. En route to Kuaotunu (52km from Colville), a turn-off at Te Rerenga after 15km leads to Whangapoua (6km). From there is a walking track (one hour return) to New Chums Beach, regarded as one of NZ's finest beaches.

- - - - - - - - - - - - - - -

⑤ Kuaotunu (p109)

Located at the end of a sweeping beach – with views of the Mercury

Islands on the near horizon – Kuaotunu is an interesting holiday village with a fine **cafe and art gallery**, and access on scenic unsealed roads to the nearby beaches of **Otama** and **Opito**. Departing Kuaotunu by Blackjack Rd, Otama is 3.5km away and reached by a winding road over a spectacular headland. Dunes fringe the sandy arc of the beach, and a further 6km on lies Opito, more populated but arguably even more spectacular. Both beaches are good for a swim before you return to Kuaotunu.

Hot Water Beach (p44)

The Drive » From Kuaotunu it's an easy 15km drive on SH25 to Whitianga. The view coming down off the final hill towards Whitianga's Buffalo Beach is spectacular.

- - - - - - - - - -

❻ Whitianga (p110)

Whitianga's big attractions are the sandy beaches of **Mercury Bay**, and diving, boating and kayaking in the nearby **Te Whanganui-A-Hei Marine Reserve**. The pretty harbour is also a base for game fishing, especially marlin and tuna between January and March. North of the harbour, **Buffalo Beach** stretches along Mercury Bay, and the town is a magnet for holidaymakers throughout summer. The legendary Polynesian seafarer Kupe is believed to have landed near here around AD 950, and the **Mercury Bay Museum** (☎07-866 0730; www.mercurybay museum.co.nz; 11a The Esplanade; adult/child $7.50/50¢; ◷10am-4pm) commemorates his visit and that of British maritime explorer Captain James Cook in 1769. Whitianga is a fast-growing town and has some of the peninsula's best restaurants. For a relaxing break from driving, book a spa session at the **Lost Spring** (☎07-866 0456; www.thelostspring.co.nz; 121a Cook Dr; per 90min/day $38/68; ◷10.30am-6pm Sun-Fri, to 8pm Sat), a thermal complex comprising a series of hot pools in a lush jungle-like setting complete with an erupting volcano.

The Drive » Depart south on SH25, skirting Whitianga Harbour to the east. Stay on SH25 to Whenuakite (26km), and turn left into Hot Water Beach Rd. After 5km, veer left onto Link Rd for 3km, and then turn right onto Hahei Beach Rd to Hahei (2km).

DETOUR:
FAR NORTH COROMANDEL

Start: ④ Colville

The rugged northernmost tip of the Coromandel Peninsula is well worth the effort required to reach it. The best time to visit is summer (December to February), when the gravel roads are dry and the pohutukawa trees are in their crimson glory.

Three kilometres north of Colville at **Whangaahei**, the sealed road turns to gravel and splits to straddle each side of the peninsula. Following the west coast, ancient pohutukawa spread overhead as you pass turquoise waters and stony beaches. The small DOC-run **Fantail Bay campsite** (☎07-866 6685; www.doc.govt.nz; Port Jackson Rd; adult/child $10/5), 23km north of Colville, has running water and a couple of long-drop toilets under the shade of puriri trees. Another 7km brings you to the **Port Jackson campsite** (☎07-866 6932; www.doc.govt.nz; Port Jackson Rd; adult/child $10/5), a larger DOC site right on the beach. There's a spectacular **lookout** about 4km further on, where a metal dish identifies the various islands on the horizon. **Great Barrier Island** is only 20km away, looking every part the extension of the Coromandel Peninsula that it once was. The road stops at **Fletcher Bay** – a magical land's end. Although it's only 37km from Colville, allow an hour for the drive.

Note there is no road linking Fletcher Bay with the east coast of the peninsula, so you need to return to Whangaahei 3km north of Colville, before branching left to return to Coromandel Town via a spectacular east coast road taking in **Waikawau** and **Kennedy Bay**. Sections of this road are unsealed gravel.

For the entire journey north from Colville to Fletcher Bay, back south to Whangaahei, and then around the east coast back to Coromandel Town, allow around four to five hours of driving time. For the Coromandel Town north to Colville section, add around 30 minutes.

TRIP HIGHLIGHT

❼ Hahei (p112)

A sleepy holiday town that explodes with visitors across summer – especially during school holidays – Hahei is located close to **Cathedral Cove**. The cove's gigantic **stone arch** and natural **waterfall shower** is best enjoyed early or late in the day to avoid the tourist buses and the worst of the hordes. From the car park, 1km north of Hahei, it's a rolling walk of 30 to 40 minutes to the cove. On the way there's rocky **Gemstone Bay**, which has a snorkelling trail where you could see big snapper, crayfish and stingrays, and sandy **Stingray Bay**. The **Cathedral Cove Water Taxi** (☎027 919 0563; www.cathedralcovewatertaxi.co.nz; return/one-way adult $25/15, child $15/10; ☺every 30min) runs frequent waterborne transport from Hahei Beach to the cove, a good idea to avoid the often busy car park. During the height of summer, a shuttle bus also runs from Hahei to the beginning of the track to the cove.

The Drive » From Hahei, depart on Hahei Beach Rd (2km) for Link Rd, turn left on Link Rd and continue for around 3km, then left onto Hot Water Beach Rd to Hot Water Beach (3km).

TRIP HIGHLIGHT

❽ Hot Water Beach (p113)

Hot Water Beach is extraordinary. For two hours either side of low tide, you can access an area of sand in front of a rocky outcrop at the middle of the beach where hot water oozes up from beneath the surface. Bring a spade, dig a hole and you've got a personal spa pool. Spades ($5) can be hired from the **Hot Water Beach Store** (☎07-866 3006; Pye Pl; ⊗9am-5pm), and local tourist information centres list tide schedules so you know when to rock up with scores of other fans of natural jacuzzis.

Note the car park outside the Hot Water Beach Store is pay and display, and it's enforced quite rigorously. Alternatively, park at the larger (free) car park before you get to the beach proper, and walk along the beach for a few hundred metres. Be aware that Hot Water Beach has dangerous rips, especially in front of the main thermal area. It's actually one of NZ's most dangerous beaches

in terms of drowning numbers, but this is potentially skewed by the huge number of tourists flocking here. Regardless, swimming is definitely not safe if lifeguards aren't on patrol, and when they are on duty always swim between the flags.

The Drive » From Hot Water Beach, return by Hot Water Beach Rd to SH25 at Whenuakite, and continue south to Whangamata, 59km from

EXPLORING THE TE WHANGANUI-A-HEI MARINE RESERVE

Departing from either Whitianga Harbour or from Hahei, local operators provide exciting and scenic access to the beautiful 840 hectares of the Te Whanganui-A-Hei Marine Reserve and around the surrounding coastline of Mercury Bay. The reserve was gazetted in 1992 and is centred on Cathedral Cove (Whanganui-A-Hei in Māori).

Hahei Explorer (☎07-866 3910; www.haheiexplorer.co.nz; adult/child $85/50) Hour-long jetboat rides touring the coast.

Cathedral Cove Sea Kayaking (☎07-866 3877; www.seakayaktours.co.nz; 88 Hahei Beach Rd; half-/full day $105/170; ⊗8.45am & 1.30pm) Guided kayaking trips around the rock arches, caves and islands in the Cathedral Cove and Mercury Bay area. The Remote Coast Tour heads the other way when conditions permit, visiting caves, blowholes and a long tunnel.

Banana Boat (☎07-866 5617; www.facebook.com/bananaboatwhitianga; rides $10-35; ⊗26 Dec-31 Jan) Monkey around in Mercury Bay on the bright-yellow motorised Banana Boat – or split to Cathedral Cove.

Glass Bottom Boat (☎07-867 1962; www.glassbottomboatwhitianga.co.nz; adult/child $95/50) Two-hour bottom-gazing tours exploring the Te Whanganui-A-Hei Marine Reserve.

Cave Cruzer (☎07-866 0611; www.cavecruzer.co.nz; adult/child 1hr $50/30, 2hr $75/40) Tours on a rigid-hull inflatable.

Ocean Leopard (☎0800 843 8687; www.oceanleopardtours.co.nz; adult/child $80/45; ⊗10.30pm, 1.30pm & 4pm) Two-hour trips around coastal scenery, naturally including Cathedral Cove. The boat has a handy canopy for sun protection, and a one-hour 'Whirlwind Tour' is also on offer.

Whitianga Adventures (☎0800 806 060; www.whitianga-adventures.co.nz; adult/child $75/45) A two-hour Sea Cave Adventure in an inflatable.

Windborne (☎027 475 2411; www.windborne.co.nz; day sail $95; ⊗Dec-Apr) Day sails in a 19m, 1928 schooner.

COROMANDEL CRAFT BEER

Yes, the Kiwi craft beer revolution has washed up on the pristine waters of Mercury Bay, and two excellent breweries are located near Hahei and Hot Water Beach. Good cafes and restaurants around the Coromandel Peninsula also stock beers from the Pour House and Hot Water Brewing Co.

Home base for the Coromandel Brewing Company, **Pour House** (www.coromandelbrewingcompany.co.nz; 7 Grange Rd; ⊙11am-11pm) in Hahei regularly features around five of its beers in a modern ambience. Platters of meat, cheese and local seafood combine with decent pizzas in the beer garden. Our favourite brew is the Code Red Irish Ale.

Located at the Sea Breeze Holiday Park in Whenuakite, **Hot Water Brewing Co** (✆07-866 3830; www.hotwaterbrewingco.com; Sea Breeze Holiday Park, 1043 SH25, Whenuakite; ⊙11am-late) is a modern craft brewery with lots of outdoor seating. Standout brews include the hoppy Kauri Falls Pale Ale and the robust Walkers Porter. Platters and pizzas make it easy to order another beer, and the lamb burger is deservedly famous around these parts. Ask if the superb Barley Wine is available.

Hot Water Beach. En route at Tairua, a steep 15-minute walk to the summit of Paaku offers great harbour views across to Pauanui. At Opoutere, the Wharekawa Wildlife Refuge is a breeding ground for the endangered NZ dotterel.

9 Whangamata (p113)

Outside of summer, 'Whanga' is a genteel seaside town (population 3560), but over Christmas, New Year and other key holiday periods, it can be a much more energetic spot, and the population swells to around 40,000 with holidaymakers from Auckland and Hamilton.

It's an excellent surf beach, and a popular destination for kayaking and paddle boarding is **Whenuakura (Donut) Island**, around 1km from the beach. There's also good snorkelling at **Hauturu (Clarke) Island**. Note that in an effort to boost the islands' status as wildlife sanctuaries, landing on them is not permitted. Boating around the islands is allowed, however. The experienced team at **SurfSup** (✆021 217 1201; www.surfsupwhangamata.com; 101b Winifred Ave; hire half-/full-day surfboard $30/50, kayak from $40/60, 1/2hr paddle board $20/30) offer

paddle-boarding and surfing lessons, and also run daily kayaking and paddle-boarding tours to Whenuakura from December to March.

The Drive » From Whangamata, SH25 continues its meandering route south to Waihi (30km).

TRIP HIGHLIGHT

10 Waihi (p114)

Gold and silver have been dragged out of Waihi's Martha Mine (NZ's richest) since 1878, and Seddon St, the town's main street, has interesting sculptures and information panels about Waihi's golden legacy. The superb **Gold Discovery Centre** (✆07-863 9015; www.golddiscoverycentre. co.nz; 126 Seddon St; adult/child $25/12; ⊙9am-5pm, to 4pm in winter) reveals the area's gold-mining past, present and future through interactive displays, focusing on the personal and poignant to tell interesting stories. Holograms and short movies both feature, drawing visitors in and informing them through entertainment. Good luck in taking on the grizzled miner at 'virtual' Two-Up (a gambling game using coins). Atmospherically lit at night, the skeleton of a derelict **Cornish Pumphouse** (1904) is the town's main landmark. From here the **Pit Rim Walkway** has fascinating views into the 250m-deep **Martha Mine**. To get down into the spectacular mine, join a 1½-hour excursion with **Waihi Gold Mine Tours** (☏07-863 9015; www.golddiscovery-centre.co.nz/tours; 126 Seddon St, Gold Discovery Centre; adult/child $34/17; ⏱10am & 12.30pm daily, additional tours in summer), departing from the Gold Discovery Centre.

The Drive >> Take SH2 south out of Waihi and turn left into Waihi Beach Rd after 3km.

- - - - - - - - - - - -

⓫ Waihi Beach (p114)

Separated from Waihi township by 11km of prime Waikato farmland, this low sandy surf beach stretches 9km to **Bowentown** on the northern limits of Tauranga Harbour. As well as being a prime summertime destination for the good people of Hamilton, Waihi Beach is also a growing foodie hot spot with a number of fine little cafes; even the pub has had a makeover and attracts locals and weekenders alike.

HAURAKI RAIL TRAIL

From Waihi township, an excellent day excursion is to combine a train ride, on the heritage **Goldfields Railway** (☏07-863 8251; www.waihirail.co.nz; 30 Wrigley St, Waihi; adult/child return $18/10, bikes $2 extra per route; ⏱departs Waihi 10am, 11.45am & 1.45pm Sat, Sun & public holidays), with a few hours' cycling part of the popular **Hauraki Rail Trail** through the scenic **Karangahake Gorge**. Bikes can be rented at the railway's terminus in the gorge, the **Waikino Station Cafe** (☏07-863 8640; www.waikinostationcafe.co.nz; SH2; mains $10-18; ⏱9.30am-3pm), or at **Waihi Bicycle Hire** (☏07-863 8418; www.waihibicyclehire.co.nz; 25 Seddon St, Waihi; bike hire half-/full day from $30/40; ⏱8am-5pm) in town and then carried on the train. This part of the Hauraki Rail Trail is spectacular as it winds on a gentle gradient through a beautiful river valley. Book ahead for lunch at **Bistro at the Falls Retreat** (☏07-863 8770; www.fallsretreat.co.nz; 25 Waitawheta Rd; pizzas $20-24, mains $25-28; ⏱10am-10pm), located in a cosy wooden cottage in the heart of a sun-dappled forest. Gourmet pizzas and rustic meat dishes emerge from the wood-fired oven on a regular basis, and there's a great little playground for children.

See www.haurakirailtrail.co.nz for detailed information, including trail maps and recommendations for other day rides on this popular cycle route linking Thames to the towns of Paeroa, Te Aroha and Waihi.

If you want to stretch your legs on more than the flat kilometres of golden beach, a good walk from the northern end of the beach leads to Orokawa Beach, 45 minutes away around the coastal headlands. In summer when the beachside pohutukawas are flowering there is no finer Coromandel sight than scarlet trees, white sand and turquoise water.

Waiheke Island Escape

4

An hour from the city, Auckland's favourite Hauraki Gulf island combines vineyard restaurants, active adventure and a thriving art scene, with beaches and coves definitely worth discovering.

TRIP HIGHLIGHTS

17 km

Onetangi Beach
Stroll or swim along this sandy arc

Oneroa

⑤

Onetangi

⑧

Te Whau Point
FINISH

Auckland
(18km)
START

⑥

EcoZip Adventures
Soar about vineyards and pristine native forest

54 km

Man O' War Bay
Negotiate winding roads to this waterfront winery

30 km

2 DAYS
62KM / 38 MILES

GREAT FOR...

BEST TIME TO GO

February to April but try and avoid busy weekends and public holidays.

 ESSENTIAL PHOTO

Being launched onto the zipline at EcoZip Adventures.

 BEST FOR FOODIES

A leisurely lunch at a top vineyard restaurant.

4 Waiheke Island Escape

Tantalisingly close to Auckland and blessed with its own warm, dry microclimate, blissful Waiheke Island has long been a favourite escape for both city dwellers and travellers. On the island's landward side, emerald waters lap at rocky bays, while its ocean flank has some of the region's best sandy beaches. Vineyards evoking a South Pacific spin on Tuscany or the south of France are other sybaritic diversions.

1 Auckland (p58)

One of the world's most beautiful harbour cities, Auckland is the gateway to the islands of the Hauraki Gulf – see its highlights on our three-hour walking tour (p80). Regular ferries leave from downtown Auckland and other locations around the city to islands promising wine, art, walking and adventure.

The Drive » From Auckland, Sealink (www.sealink.co.nz) runs car ferries (adult/child/car return $36.50/20/168) to Kennedy Point on Waiheke

Island. Most leave from Half Moon Bay in east Auckland (45 to 60 minutes), but some depart from Wynyard Wharf in the city (60 to 80 minutes). From Kennedy Point to Oneroa, Waiheke's main town, is 3km.

2 Oneroa (p73)

Waiheke's main settlement comprises a relaxed main street dotted with cafes, restaurants, gift shops and local stores. **Oneroa Beach** and the pretty cove of **Little Oneroa** nearby are both good for swimming. In town, attractions are conveniently centred on the **Waiheke Island Artworks** (2 Korora Rd;) complex, and include the **Waiheke Community Art Gallery** (☏09-372 9907; www.waihekeartgallery.org. nz; ☺10am-4pm) – featuring local artists and an excellent gift shop – and **Whittaker's Musical Museum** (☏09-372 5573; www. musicalmuseum.org; suggested donation $5; ☺1-4pm, live shows 1.30pm Sat), with afternoon concerts played on heritage instruments. Drop in at the **Waiheke Wine Centre** (☏09-372 6139; www.waihekewinecentre. com; 153 Oceanview Rd; ☺9.30am-7.30pm Mon-Thu, to 8pm Fri & Sat, from 11am Sun) featuring wine from all of Waiheke's 30-plus vineyards.

The Drive » Leave Oneroa on Oceanview Rd – up the hill – and after 500m turn left into Church Bay Rd. Look for the small brown sign indicating 'Wineries'. Continue on Church Bay Rd for 2.5km to Mudbrick.

3 Church Bay

With spectacular views to central Auckland – including the imposing profile of the **Sky Tower** – the two vineyards above pretty Church Bay are deservedly very popular. Auckland and the gulf are at their glistening best when viewed from the picturesque veranda at **Mudbrick** (☏09-372 9050; www.mudbrick.co.nz; 126 Church Bay Rd; mains $46-49; ☺11.30am-3.30pm & 6-10.30pm). The pretty formal gardens make it popular for weddings, which periodically take over the restaurant (be sure to book ahead). The winery also offers tastings (from $10, 10am to 4pm). One kilometre back down the hill towards Oneroa, **Cable Bay** (☏09-372 5889; www.cablebay. co.nz; 12 Nick Johnstone Dr; mains $42-44; ☺noon-3pm Tue-Sun, 6pm-late Tue-Sat;) features contemporary architecture and more stunning vistas. There are two good restaurants, and wine tasting ($10 for five wines, 11am to 5pm daily) takes place in a stylish tasting room.

The Drive » Return to Oceanview Rd via Church Bay Rd and continue for 2.7km before

🔗 LINK YOUR TRIP

1 Northland & the Bay of Islands
More great beaches and discovering NZ's shared Māori and European heritage.

2 East & West Coast Explorer
More food- and wine-related fun amid Aucklanders' favourite day trips.

Cactus Bay

Man O' War Bay 6

Te Haahi-Goodwin Reserve

Omaru Bay

Connells Bay 7

turning right into Surfdale Rd. Continue on this road for 5.5km until you see a sign for 'Wild on Waiheke' on your left.

---

4 Onetangi (p73)

Three Waiheke attractions are handily adjacent amid Onetangi's rural ambience. **Wild on Waiheke** (☎09-372 3434; www.wildonwaiheke.co.nz; 82 Onetangi Rd; tastings per beer or wine $2-3; ⏰11am-4pm Thu-Sun, daily in summer; 👶) combines a winery and a microbrewery with archery, laser clay shooting, *pétanque* and a giant chessboard. A secondary route leads to nearby **Stonyridge** (☎09-372 8822; www.stonyridge. com; 80 Onetangi Rd; tastings per wine $4-18; ⏰11.30am-5pm; 📶). Waiheke's most famous vineyard is home to world-beating reds, an atmospheric cafe, and tours ($10 including tastings of two wines, 30 minutes, 11.30am Saturday and Sunday). Combine a bottle with one of Stonyridge's deli platters and retreat to a garden cabana. Another nearby unsealed road meanders to the **Shed at Te Motu** (p78). Te Motu is most famous for stellar Bordeaux-style red wines, and sophisticated shared plates imbued with global culinary influences are served under umbrellas in the restaurant's rustic courtyard.

The Drive » Continue east along Onetangi Rd for 2.5km to Onetangi Beach.

TRIP HIGHLIGHT

5 Onetangi Beach (p73)

Waiheke's best beach is a 1.9m sandy arc bookended by forested headlands. The humble baches (simple holiday homes) of earlier decades have now largely been replaced by million-dollar homes with ocean views, but the beach is still accessible to all. It's a wonderful spot for a leisurely stroll, and the gently rolling breakers coming in from the Hauraki Gulf are often perfect for bodysurfing. At the beach's eastern end, **Charlie Farley's** (☎09-372 4106; www.charlie farleys.co.nz; 21 The Strand, Onetangi; ⏰8.30am-late) is the locals' favourite, and the pohutukawa-tree-shaded deck is a top spot for a New Zealand craft beer or a leisurely lunch or dinner.

The Drive » Return to Onetangi Rd and turn left after 300m into Waiheke Rd. Continue for 4.5km before turning left into Man O' War Bay Rd. Travel for 9km on an unsealed road with superb ocean views to Man O' War Bay. This road is narrow and winding in parts so take extra care.

OLIVER STREWE/GETTY IMAGES ©

TRIP HIGHLIGHT

6 Man O' War Bay (p73)

Yes, the drive to Man O' War Bay on unsealed roads can be bumpy, but it is definitely one of Waiheke's most beautiful spots. The beach is great for swimming, a slender wooden wharf stretches

Gregor Kregar's *Vanish* sculpture, Connells Bay

into the water, and there are great views of nearby **Pakatoa** and **Rotoroa Islands**. An essential island experience is to settle in with a tasting platter at the beachfront tasting room of the **Man O' War vineyard** (☎09-372 9678; www.manowarvineyards. co.nz; 725 Man O' War Bay Rd; ◷11am-6pm Dec-Feb, to 4.30pm Mar-Nov). The Valhalla chardonnay is

an outstanding wine, and the rosé is highly recommended with tapas including charcuterie, cheeses and plump Waiheke olives. Beer fans can cool down with Man O' War's very own 'Great Harry' lager.

The Drive » Leave Man O' War Bay on the unsealed road in front of the beach. Look for the heritage church that is used for summer weddings. Continue

over the beach's southern headland for 6km before turning left down to Connells Bay.

– – – – – – – – – – – – –

7 Connells Bay

Reached by a road in the island's remote southeastern corner, this private sculpture park in beautiful **Connells Bay** (☎09-372 8957; www. connellsbay.co.nz; 142 Cowes Bay Rd; adult/child $30/15;

**LOCAL KNOWLEDGE:
TIME FOR AN
ICE CREAM...**

Before school, after school, and on weekdays and weekends, Waiheke locals crowd the funky shipping-container garden at **Island Gelato** (📞021 536 860; www.islandgelato.co.nz; 1 Oceanview Rd, Oneroa; ice cream from $5; 🕑7.30am-5pm Sun-Thu, to 8pm Fri & Sat) for delicious ice cream, coffee and bagels. Seasonal ice-cream flavours shine, including our favourite, the zingy kaffir-lime-and-coconut sorbet. You'll find all this irresistible goodness at the bottom end of Oneroa village.

🕑by appointment Nov-Mar) features a stellar roster of NZ artists. Around 30 different works punctuate the coastal terrain. Admission is by way of a two-hour guided tour, so visitors need to book ahead. Note the park is only open from late October to mid-April.

The Drive » Continue for 1.5km south on Cowes Bay Rd to the intersection with Orapiu Rd. Turn right into Orapiu Rd – this section is sealed again – and continue for 14km via Waiheke Rd to Onetangi Rd. Turn left on Onetangi Rd before turning left into Trig Hill Rd for 2km. Look for the sign to EcoZip Adventures.

TRIP HIGHLIGHT

8 EcoZip Adventures

Soar on a zipline above vineyards and native forest on Waiheke Island's most exciting experience. Three separate 200m-long stretches add up to a thrilling ride at **EcoZip Adventures** (📞09-372 5646; www.ecozipadventures.co.nz; 150 Trig Hill Rd; adult/child/family $119/79/317; 🕑9am-5pm), but it's definitely a soft adventure suitable for most travellers. Look out to the skyline of Auckland's CBD as you're whizzing through the island air. Following the zipline, there is a pleasant 1.4km walk through the pristine forest. Costs include free transfers from Matiatia Wharf or Oneroa if you don't have your own transport. A few hundred metres further along Trig Hill Rd, **Peacock Sky** (📞09-950 4386; www.peacocksky.co.nz; 152 Trig Hill Rd; 🕑noon-5pm)

combines a rustic vineyard ambience with wine tasting (from $3), and main dishes ($25 to $32) and shared platters ($40) combining local produce and international flavours.

The Drive » Return via Trig Hill Rd to Onetangi Rd and continue left for 2.2km. Turn left into O'Brien Rd and then right onto Te Whau Dr for 4km out to the end of the Te Whau peninsula.

9 Te Whau Point

Perched on the end of the peninsula, the restaurant at **Te Whau** (📞09-372 7191; www.tewhau.com; 218 Te Whau Dr; mains $40-42; 🕑11am-5pm daily & 6.30-11pm Thu-Sat Dec & Jan, 11am-5pm Wed-Mon & 6.30-11pm Sat Feb-Easter, 11am-4.30pm Fri-Sun & 6.30-11pm Sat Easter-Nov) has exceptional views, food and service, and one of NZ's finest wine lists. The attached tasting room offers samples of its own impressive Bordeaux blends (11am to 5pm, four tastes for $12). En route stop at **Azurro Groves** (📞09-372 2700; www.azzurogroves.com; 152 Te Whau Dr; 🕑11.30am-3.30pm, reduced hours Jun-Aug) to taste (and purchase) some of Waiheke's finest olive oils.

Destinations

Auckland & Around (p58)

Cradled by two harbours, cosmopolitan Auckland isn't your average metropolis. Surrounded by wine regions, wild beaches and beautiful Waiheke Island, it's regularly rated one of the world's most liveable cities.

Bay of Islands & Northland (p82)

Turquoise waters lapping pretty bays, dolphins frolicking at the bows of boats, pods of orcas gliding gracefully by: these are the kinds of experiences that the Bay of Islands delivers so well.

Coromandel Peninsula (p105)

A favourite destination of Aucklanders for decades, the Coromandel Peninsula conceals superb beaches and hidden coves.

Detail of Māori ancestral home, Auckland Museum (p59)
IAN TROWER/GETTY IMAGES ©

Paris may be the city of love, but Auckland is the city of many lovers, according to its Māori name, Tāmaki Makaurau. Those lovers so desired this place that they fought over it for centuries.

Auckland & Around

AUCKLAND

Auckland is a city of volcanoes, with the ridges of lava flows forming its main thoroughfares and its many cones providing islands of green within the sea of suburbs. As well as being by far the largest, it's also the most multicultural of NZ's cities. A sizeable Asian community rubs shoulders with the biggest Polynesian population of any city in the world.

It's hard to imagine a more geographically blessed city. Its two harbours frame a narrow isthmus punctuated by volcanic cones and surrounded by fertile farmland. From any of its numerous vantage points you'll be surprised how close the Tasman Sea and Pacific Ocean come to kissing and forming a new island.

Whether it's the ruggedly beautiful west-coast surf beaches, or the glistening Hauraki Gulf with its myriad islands, the water's never far away. And within an hour's drive from the city's high-rise heart, there are dense tracts of rainforest, thermal springs, wineries and wildlife reserves. No wonder Auckland is regularly rated one of the world's top cities for quality of life and liveability.

The traditional Kiwi aspiration for a free-standing house on a quarter-acre section has resulted in a vast, sprawling city. The CBD was long ago abandoned to commerce, and inner-city apartment living has only recently caught on. While geography has been kind, city planning has been less so.

Unbridled and ill-conceived development has left the centre of the city with plenty of architectural embarrassments. To get under Auckland's skin you're best to head to the streets of Victorian and Edwardian villas in hip inner-city suburbs such as Ponsonby, Grey Lynn, Kingsland and Mt Eden.

◉ Sights

★ Auckland Art Gallery   GALLERY
(☑ 09-379 1349; www.aucklandartgallery.com; cnr Kitchener & Wellesley Sts; ⊙10am-5pm) **FREE**
Following a significant 2011 refurbishment, Auckland's premier art repository now has a striking glass-and-wood atrium grafted onto its 1887 French-chateau frame. It showcases the best of NZ art, along with important works by Pieter Bruegel the Younger, Guido Reni, Picasso, Cézanne, Gauguin and Matisse. Highlights include the intimate 19th-century portraits of tattooed Māori subjects by Charles Goldie, and the starkly dramatic text-scrawled canvasses of Colin McCahon.

Free tours depart from the foyer daily at 11.30am and 1.30pm.

Albert Park   PARK
(Princes St) Hugging the hill on the city's eastern flank, Albert Park is a charming Victorian formal garden overrun by students from the neighbouring University of Auckland during term time. The park was once part of the Albert Barracks (1847), a fortification that enclosed 9 hectares during the New Zealand Wars. A portion of the original

barracks wall survives at the centre of the university campus.

Sky Tower
TOWER

(☑09-363 6000; www.skycityauckland.co.nz; cnr Federal & Victoria Sts; adult/child $28/11; ☺8.30am-10.30pm) ✒ The impossible-to-miss Sky Tower looks like a giant hypodermic giving a fix to the heavens. Spectacular lighting renders it space age at night and the colours change for special events. At 328m it is the southern hemisphere's tallest structure. A lift takes you up to the observation decks in 40 stomach-lurching seconds; look down through the glass floor panels if you're after an extra kick. Consider visiting at sunset and having a drink in the Sky Lounge Cafe & Bar.

St Patrick's Cathedral
CHURCH

(☑09-303 4509; www.stpatricks.org.nz; 43 Wyndham St; ☺7am-7pm) Auckland's Catholic cathedral (1907) is one of the city's loveliest buildings. Polished wood and Belgian stained glass lend warmth to the interior of the majestic Gothic Revival church. There's a historical display in the old confessional on the left-hand side.

Mt Eden
VOLCANO

(Maungawhau; 250 Mt Eden Rd) From the top of Auckland's highest volcanic cone (196m) the entire isthmus and both harbours are laid bare. The symmetrical crater (50m deep) is known as Te Ipu Kai a Mataaho (the Food Bowl of Mataaho, the god of things hidden in the ground) and is considered highly *tapu* (sacred). Do not enter it, but feel free to explore the remainder of the mountain. The remains of *pa* (fortified village) terraces and food storage pits are clearly visible.

Until recently it was possible to drive right up to the summit but concerns over erosion have led to restricted vehicle access. Paths lead up the mountain from six different directions and the walk only takes around 10 minutes, depending on your fitness.

★Auckland Museum
MUSEUM

(☑09-309 0443; www.aucklandmuseum.com; Auckland Domain, Parnell; adult/child $25/10; ☺10am-5pm) This imposing neoclassical temple (1929), capped with an impressive copper-and-glass dome (2007), dominates the Auckland Domain and is a prominent part of the Auckland skyline, especially when viewed from the harbour. Admission packages can be purchased, which incorporate a highlights tour and a Māori cultural performance ($45 to $55). The displays of Pacific Island and Māori artefacts on the museum's ground floor are essential viewing.

One Tree Hill
VOLCANO, PARK

(Maungakiekie) This volcanic cone was the isthmus' key *pa* and the greatest fortress in the country. At the top (182m) there are 360-degree views and the grave of John Logan Campbell, who gifted the land to the city in 1901 and requested that a memorial be built to the Māori people on the summit. Nearby is the stump of the last 'one tree'. Allow time to explore surrounding Cornwall Park with its mature trees and historic Acacia Cottage (1841).

Auckland Botanic Gardens
GARDENS

(☑09-267 1457; www.aucklandbotanicgardens. co.nz; 102 Hill Rd, Manurewa; ☺8am-6pm Apr-Sep, to 8pm Oct-Mar) ✒ FREE This 64-hectare park has over 10,000 plants (including threatened species), dozens of themed

---

ONE TREE TO RULE THEM ALL

Looking at One Tree Hill, your first thought will probably be 'Where's the bloody tree?'. Good question. Up until 2000 a Monterey pine stood at the top of the hill. This was a replacement for a sacred totara that was chopped down by British settlers in 1852. Māori activists first attacked the foreign usurper in 1994, finishing the job in 2000.

After much hand-wringing and consultation with local Māori and tree experts, it was finally announced in late 2015 that a grove of pohutukawa, totara and other natives would be planted on the summit. Then, in an arboreal version of the *X-Factor* the weaker performing trees will be eliminated, leaving only one tree standing by 2026.

Auckland's most beloved landmark achieved international recognition in 1987 when U2 released the song 'One Tree Hill' on their acclaimed *The Joshua Tree* album. It was only released as a single in NZ, where it went to number one for six weeks.

City Centre

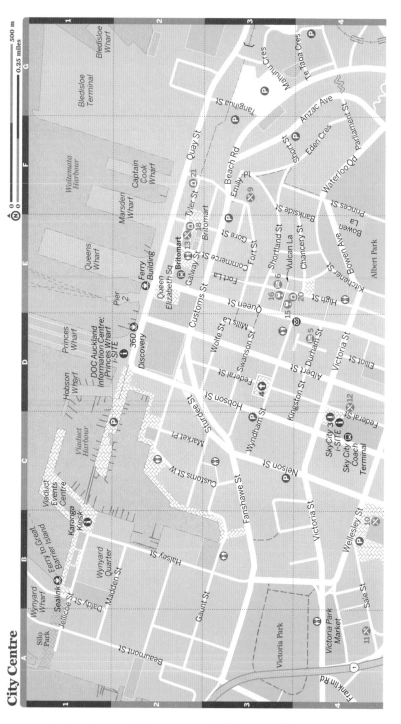

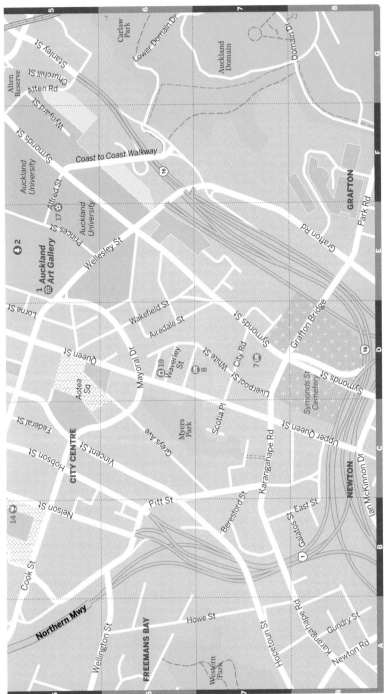

61

City Centre

gardens and an infestation of wedding parties. By car, take the Southern Motorway, exit at Manurewa and follow the signs. Otherwise take the train to Manurewa ($8, 43 minutes) and then walk along Hill Rd (1.5km).

☞ Tours

Tāmaki Hikoi CULTURAL TOUR
(☑ 021 146 9593; www.tamakihikoi.co.nz; 1/3hr $40/95) Guides from the Ngāti Whātua *iwi* (tribe) lead various Māori cultural tours, including walking and interpretation of sites such as Mt Eden and the Auckland Domain.

Big Foody Food Tour FOOD TOUR
(☑ 021 481 177, 0800 366 386; www.thebigfoody. com; per person $125-185) Small-group city tours, including visits to markets and artisan producers, and lots of tastings.

Auckland Wine Trail Tours WINE TOUR
(☑ 09-630 1540; www.winetrailtours.co.nz) Small-group tours around west Auckland wineries and the Waitakere Ranges (half/full day $125/255); further afield to Matakana ($265); or a combo of the two ($265).

Auckland Hop On,
Hop Off Explorer BUS TOUR
(☑ 0800 439 756; www.explorerbus.co.nz; adult/ child $45/20) This service departs from the Ferry Building every hour from 10am to 3pm (bus services run more frequently in summer), heading to 14 tourist sites around the city.

✯ Festivals & Events

Auckland Anniversary Day
Regatta SPORTS
(www.regatta.org.nz; ☉ Jan) The 'City of Sails' lives up to its name; held Monday of the last weekend in January.

★ Pasifika Festival CULTURAL
(www.aucklandnz.com/pasifika; ☉ Mar) Western Springs Park hosts this giant Polynesian party with cultural performances, food and craft stalls; held over a weekend in early to mid-March.

Auckland Arts Festival PERFORMING ARTS
(www.aucklandfestival.co.nz; ☉ Mar) Held over three weeks in March, this is Auckland's biggest celebration of the arts.

⬛ Sleeping

YHA Auckland International HOSTEL $
(☑ 09-302 8200; www.yha.co.nz; 5 Turner St; dm $28-31, r $99, without bathroom $90; P ⬛ ⬛) ✪ Clean and brightly painted, this 170-bed YHA has a friendly vibe, good security, a games room and lots of lockers.

CityLife HOTEL $$
(☑ 09-379 9222; www.heritagehotels.co.nz/ citylife-auckland; 171 Queen St; apt from $162; P ⬛ ⬛ ⬛) ✪ A worthy tower-block hotel offering numerous apartments over dozens of floors, ranging from studios to three-bedroom suites. Facilities include a heated lap pool, gym and valet parking. The location couldn't be more central.

Abaco on Jervois
MOTEL **$$**

(☏09-360 6850; www.abaco.co.nz; 57 Jervois Rd, Ponsonby; r/ste from $145/198; 🅿🛜) Well positioned for cafes and buses, this contemporary, neutral-toned motel has stainless-steel kitchens with dishwashers in the fancier units, and fridges and microwaves in the studios. The darker rooms downstairs are cheaper.

Quest Carlaw Park
APARTMENT **$$**

(☏09-304 0521; www.questcarlawpark.co.nz; 15 Nicholls Lane; apt from $189; 🅿@🛜) ✈ It's in an odd spot but this set of smart, modern apartments is handy for Parnell, the city and the Domain, and if you've got a car, you're practically on the motorway.

Quality Hotel Parnell
HOTEL **$$**

(☏09-303 3789; www.theparnell.co.nz; 10-20 Gladstone Rd; r from $138; 🅿🛜) More than 100 motel rooms and units are available in this renovated complex. The newer north wing has great harbour views.

Devonport Motel
MOTEL **$$**

(☏09-445 1010; www.devonportmotel.co.nz; 11 Buchanan St, Devonport; r $160; 🅿🛜) This mini-imotel has two units in the tidy back garden. They're modern, clean, self-contained and in a quiet location close to Devonport's attractions.

★ Hotel DeBrett
BOUTIQUE HOTEL **$$$**

(☏09-925 9000; www.hoteldebrett.com; 2 High St; r from $330; 🛜) This hip historic hotel has been zhooshed up with stripy carpets and clever designer touches in every nook of the 25 extremely comfortable rooms. Prices include a continental breakfast, free unlimited wi-fi and a pre-dinner drink.

★ Ascot Parnell
B&B **$$$**

(☏09-309 9012; www.ascotparnell.com; 32 St Stephens Ave, Parnell; r $255-325; 🅿@🛜🛗) The Ascot's three luxurious bedrooms share a spacious apartment in a modern midrise block. You're in no danger of stumbling into the owners' private space; they have a completely separate apartment next door. The largest room grabs all of the harbour views but you can enjoy the same vista from the large terrace leading off the communal living area.

Great Ponsonby Arthotel
B&B **$$$**

(☏09-376 5989; www.greatpons.co.nz; 30 Ponsonby Tce; r $250-400; 🅿🛜) ✈ In a quiet cul-de-sac near Ponsonby Rd, this deceptively spacious Victorian villa has gregarious hosts, impressive sustainability practices and great breakfasts. Studio apartments open onto an attractive rear courtyard. Rates include breakfast.

Langham
HOTEL **$$$**

(☏09-379 5132; www.auckland.langhamhotels.co.nz; 83 Symonds St; r from $275; 🅿@🛜🛗) ✈ The Langham's service is typically faultless, the beds are heavenly, and its day spa is one of Auckland's best.

Eden Villa
B&B **$$$**

(☏09-630 1165; www.edenvilla.co.nz; 16 Poronui St, Mt Eden; r $250) These pretty wooden villas are what Auckland's leafy inner suburbs are all about. This one has three comfortable en suite bedrooms, a pleasantly old-fashioned ambience and charming hosts who prepare a good cooked breakfast. We prefer the room at the rear, which has the original bathtub and views straight over the garden to Mt Eden itself.

✖ Eating

★ Best Ugly Bagels
BAKERY, CAFE **$**

(☏09-366 3926; www.bestugly.co.nz; City Works Depot, 90 Wellesley St; filled bagels $5-12; ⊙7am-3am; ✈) Hand rolled, boiled and wood-fired, Best Ugly's bagels are a thing of beauty. Call into its super-hip bakery in a converted heavy vehicle workshop and order one

---

ESSENTIAL AUCKLAND
....

Eat Amid the diverse and cosmopolitan scene of Ponsonby Central.

Drink World-class wine at a Waiheke vineyard.

Read *Under the Mountain* (1979) – Maurice Gee's teenage tale of slimy things lurking under Auckland's volcanoes.

Listen to *Pure Heroine* (2013) – Savvy lyrics and beats from Devonport's very own Lorde.

Watch *The Piano* (1993) – Multiple Oscar winner filmed at Karekare Beach.

Festival Pasifika

Online www.aucklandnz.com; www.lonelyplanet.com/new-zealand/auckland

Area code ☏09

stuffed with pastrami, bacon, smoked salmon or a variety of vegetarian fillings. Or just ask for a cinnamon bagel slathered with cream cheese and jam. The coffee is killer, too.

★ **Depot** MODERN NZ **$$**
(www.eatatdepot.co.nz; 86 Federal St; dishes $16-34; ⊘7am-late) TV chef Al Brown's popular eatery offers first-rate comfort food in informal surrounds (communal tables, butcher tiles and a constant buzz). Dishes are designed to be shared, and a pair of clever shuckers serve up the city's freshest clams and oysters. It doesn't take bookings, so get there early or expect to wait.

★ **Beirut** LEBANESE **$$**
(☑09-367 6882; www.beirut.co.nz; 85 Fort St; mains $26-29; ⊘7am-late Mon-Fri, 5pm-late Sat) Sacking curtains and industrial decor don't necessarily scream out Lebanese, but the sophisticated, punchy flavours bursting from the plates at this wonderful new restaurant certainly do. The cocktails are nearly as exciting as the food – and that's saying something.

★ **Ortolana** ITALIAN **$$**
(www.ortolana.co.nz; 33 Tyler St, Britomart; mains $25-29; ⊘7am-11pm) Mediterranean and regional Italian flavours are showcased at this stylish restaurant. Dishes are as artfully arranged as they are delicious, and much of the produce comes from the owners' small farm in rural west Auckland. Some of the sweets come from its sister patisserie, the very fabulous Milse, next door. It doesn't take bookings.

DON'T MISS

NORTH SHORE BEACHES
....
Fine swimming beaches stretch from North Head to Long Bay. The gulf islands shelter them from strong surf, making them safe for supervised children. Aim for high tide unless you fancy a lengthy walk to waist-deep water. Cheltenham Beach is a short walk from Devonport. Takapuna Beach, closest to the Harbour Bridge, is Auckland's answer to Bondi and the most built up. Nearby St Leonards Beach, popular with gay men, requires clambering over rocks at high tide.

★ **Saan** THAI **$$**
(☑09-320 4237; www.saan.co.nz; 160 Ponsonby Rd, Ponsonby; dishes $14-28; ⊘5pm-late Mon & Tue, noon-late Wed-Sun) Hot in both senses of the word, this super-fashionable restaurant focuses on the fiery cuisine of the Isaan and Lanna regions of northern Thailand. The menu is conveniently sorted from least to most spicy and split into smaller and larger dishes for sharing. Be sure to order the soft-shell crab; it's truly exceptional.

★ **Sugar Club** MODERN NZ **$$$**
(☑09-363 6365; www.thesugarclub.co.nz; L53 Sky Tower, Federal St; 2-/3-/4-/5-course lunch $56/70/84/98, 3-/4-/5-/6-course dinner $90/108/118/128; ⊘noon-2.30pm Wed-Sun & 5.30-9.30pm daily) It pays not to expect too much from restaurants stuck up towers, but when the executive chef is NZ's most famous culinary son, Peter Gordon, heralded in the UK as the 'godfather of fusion cuisine', you can comfortably raise your expectations. Gordon's meticulously constructed, flavour-filled dishes compete with the stupendous views and come out on top.

★ **Clooney** MODERN NZ **$$$**
(☑09-358 1702; www.clooney.co.nz; 33 Sale St, Freemans Bay; 2-/3-/7-course menu $80/100/150; ⊘6pm-late Tue-Sun, noon-3pm Fri) Like the Hollywood actor of the same name, Clooney is suave, stylish and extremely sophisticated, suited up in basic black. While the taste combinations are complex, the results are faultless – which, coupled with impeccable service, puts Clooney firmly in the pricey-but-worth-it category.

★ **Sidart** MODERN NZ **$$$**
(☑09-360 2122; www.sidart.co.nz; Three Lamps Plaza, 283 Ponsonby Rd, Ponsonby; 8-course lunch $50, 5-9-course dinner $85-150; ⊘noon-2.30pm Fri, 6-11pm Tue-Sat) No one in Auckland produces creative degustations quite like Sid Sahrawat. It's food as art, food as science but, more importantly, food to fire up your taste buds, delight the brain, satisfy the stomach and put a smile on your face. The restaurant is a little hard to find, tucked away at the rear of what was once the Alhambra cinema.

🍷 Drinking & Nightlife

★ **Brothers Beer** CRAFT BEER
(☑09-366 6100; www.brothersbeer.co.nz; City Works Depot, 90 Wellesley St; ⊘noon-10pm) Our favourite Auckland beer bar combines industrial decor with 18 taps crammed with

Auckland Botanic Gardens (p59)

the Brothers' own brews and guest beers from NZ and further afield. Hundreds more bottled beers await chilling in the fridges, and bar food includes top-notch pizza. It also offers tasting flights (five small glasses for $25).

Gin Room
BAR

(www.ginroom.co.nz; L1, 12 Vulcan Lane; ⊙5pm-midnight Tue & Wed, 5pm-2am Thu, 5pm-4am Fri, 6pm-4am Sat) There's a slightly dishevelled colonial charm to this bar, discreetly tucked away above Auckland's oldest pub, which is completely in keeping with its latest incarnation as a gin palace. There's at least 50 ways to ruin mother here – ask the bar staff for advice – and that's not even counting the juniper-sozzled cocktails.

Cassette Nine
CLUB

(☑09-366 0196; www.cassettenine.com; 9 Vulcan Lane; ⊙4pm-late Tue-Fri, 6pm-late Sat) Hipsters gravitate to this eccentric bar-club for music ranging from live indie to international DJ sets.

★ Gypsy Tea Room
BAR

(☑09-361 6970; www.gypsytearoom.co.nz; 455 Richmond Rd, Grey Lynn; ⊙4-11.30pm Sun-Thu, 3pm-2am Fri & Sat) This little neighbourhood cocktail-wine bar has bohemian charm in bucketloads. Rest assured, no one comes here for tea.

★ Freida Margolis
BAR

(☑09-378 6625; www.facebook.com/freidamargolis; 440 Richmond Rd, Grey Lynn; ⊙4pm-late) Formerly a butchers – look for the Westlynn Organic Meats sign – this corner location is now a great little neighbourhood bar with a backstreets of Bogota ambience. Loyal locals sit outside with their well-behaved dogs, supping on sangria, wine and craft beer, and enjoying eclectic sounds from the owner's big vinyl collection.

★ Golden Dawn
BAR

(☑09-376 9929; www.goldendawn.co.nz; 134b Ponsonby Rd, Grey Lynn; ⊙4pm-midnight Tue-Fri, noon-midnight Sat & Sun) Occupying an old shopfront and an inviting stables yard, this hip drinking den regularly hosts happenings including DJs and live bands. There's also excellent food on offer, including pulled-pork rolls, and prawn buns with Japanese mayo and chilli. The entrance is via the unmarked door just around the corner on Richmond Rd.

☆ Entertainment

Kings Arms Tavern
LIVE MUSIC

(☑09-373 3240; www.kingsarms.co.nz; 59 France St, Newton) This heritage pub with a great beer garden is Auckland's leading small venue for local and up-and-coming international bands.

DON'T MISS

AUCKLAND VOLCANIC FIELD

Some cities think they're tough just by living in the shadow of a volcano. Auckland's built on 50 of them and, no, they're not all extinct. The last one to erupt was Rangitoto about 600 years ago and no one can predict when the next eruption will occur. Auckland's quite literally a hot spot – with a reservoir of magma 100km below, waiting to bubble to the surface. But relax: this has only happened 19 times in the last 20,000 years.

Some of Auckland's volcanoes are cones, some are filled with water and some have been completely quarried away. Moves are afoot to register the field as a World Heritage Site and protect what remains. Most of the surviving cones show evidence of terracing from when they formed a formidable series of Māori *pa* (fortified villages). The most interesting to explore are Mt Eden (p59), One Tree Hill (p59), North Head (p102) and Rangitoto, but Mt Victoria, Mt Wellington (Maungarei), Mt Albert (Owairaka), Mt Roskill (Puketāpapa), Lake Pupuke, Mt Mangere and Mt Hobson (Remuera) are also all worth a visit.

Vector Arena STADIUM
(☑ 09-358 1250; www.vectorarena.co.nz; Mahuhu Cres) Auckland's top indoor arena for major touring acts.

Auckland Town Hall CLASSICAL MUSIC
(☑ 09-309 2677; www.aucklandlive.co.nz; 305 Queen St) This elegant Edwardian venue (1911) hosts the NZ Symphony Orchestra (www.nzso.co.nz) and Auckland Philharmonia (www.apo.co.nz), among others.

Maidment Theatre THEATRE
(☑ 09-308 2383; www.maidment. auckland.ac.nz; 8 Alfred St) The University of Auckland's theatre often stages Auckland Theatre Company (www.atc.co.nz) productions.

Eden Park SPECTATOR SPORT
(☑ 09-815 5551; www.edenpark.co.nz; Reimers Ave, Mt Eden) This stadium hosts top rugby (winter) and cricket (summer) tests by the All Blacks (www.allblacks.com) and the Black Caps (www.blackcaps.co.nz), respectively. It's also the home ground of Auckland Rugby (www.aucklandrugby.co.nz), the Blues Super Rugby team (www.theblues.co.nz) and Auckland Cricket (www.aucklandcricket.co.nz). Catch the train from Britomart to Kingsland and follow the crowds.

🛍 Shopping

★ Real Groovy MUSIC
(☑ 09-302 3940; www.realgroovy.co.nz; 369 Queen St; ☺ 9am-7pm Sat-Wed, to 9pm Thu & Fri) Masses of new, secondhand and rare releases in vinyl and CD format, as well as concert tickets, giant posters, DVDs, books, magazines and clothes.

★ Unity Books BOOKS
(☑ 09-307 0731; www.unitybooks.co.nz; 19 High St; ☺ 8.30am-7pm Mon-Sat, 10am-6pm Sun) The inner city's best independent bookshop.

★ Zambesi CLOTHING
(☑ 09-303 1701; www.zambesi.co.nz; 56 Tyler St; ☺ 9.30am-6pm Mon-Sat, 11am-4pm Sun) Iconic NZ label much sought after by local and international celebs. Also in **Ponsonby** (☑ 09-360 7391; www.zambesi.co.nz; 169 Ponsonby Rd; ☺ 9.30am-6pm Mon-Sat, 11am-4pm Sun) and **Newmarket** (☑ 09-523 1000; www.zambesi .co.nz; 38 Osborne St; ☺ 9.30am-6pm Mon-Sat, 11am-4pm Sun).

Karen Walker CLOTHING
(☑ 09-309 6299; www.karenwalker.com; 18 Te Ara Tahuhu Walkway, Britomart; ☺ 10am-6pm) Join Madonna and Kirsten Dunst in wearing Walker's cool (but pricey) threads. Also in **Grey Lynn** (☑ 09-361 6723; 128a Ponsonby Rd; ☺ 10am-5.30pm Mon-Sat, 11am-4pm Sun) and **Newmarket** (☑ 09-522 4286; 6 Balm St; ☺ 10am-6pm).

ℹ Information

MEDICAL SERVICES

Auckland City Hospital (☑ 09-367 0000; www.adhb.govt.nz; 2 Park Rd, Grafton; ☺ 24hr) The city's main hospital has a dedicated accident and emergency (A&E) service.

TOURIST INFORMATION

Auckland International Airport i-SITE (☑ 09-365 9925; www.aucklandnz.com; International Arrivals Hall; ☺ 6.30am-10.30pm)

Princes Wharf i-SITE (☑ 09-365 9914; www. aucklandnz.com; 139 Quay St; ☺ 9am-5pm)

Auckland's main official information centre, incorporating the DOC Auckland Visitor Centre (☑ 09-379 6476; www.doc.govt.nz; 137 Quay St, Princes Wharf; ☺ 9am-5pm Mon-Fri, extended hours in summer).

❶ Getting There & Away

AIR

Auckland is the main international gateway to NZ, and a hub for domestic flights. **Auckland Airport** (AKL; ☑ 09-275 0789; www.aucklandairport.co.nz; Ray Emery Dr, Mangere) is 21km south of the city centre. It has separate international and domestic terminals, a 10-minute walk apart from each other via a signposted footpath; a free shuttle service operates every 15 minutes (5am to 10.30pm). Both terminals have left-luggage facilities, eateries, ATMs and car-rental desks.

Air Chathams (☑ 09-257 0261; www.airchathams.co.nz) Flies to Whakatane and the Chatham Islands.

Air New Zealand (☑ 09-357 3000; www.airnewzealand.co.nz) Flies to Kerikeri, Whangarei, Hamilton, Tauranga, Rotorua, Taupo, Gisborne, New Plymouth, Napier, Whanganui, Palmerston North, Kapati Coast, Wellington, Nelson, Blenheim, Christchurch, Queenstown and Dunedin.

Jetstar (☑ 0800 800 995; www.jetstar.com) Flies to Wellington, Christchurch, Queenstown and Dunedin.

Virgin Australia (www.virginaustralia.com) Flies to Dunedin.

CAR & CAMPERVAN

Hire

Auckland has many hire agencies around Beach Rd and Stanley St close to the city centre.

A2B (☑ 0800 545 000; www.a2b-car-rental.co.nz; 167 Beach Rd; ☺ 7am-7pm Nov-Apr, 8am-5pm May-Oct) Cheap older cars with no visible hire-car branding.

Apex Car Rentals (☑ 09-307 1063; www.apexrentals.co.nz; 156 Beach Rd; ☺ 8am-5pm)

Budget (☑ 09-976 2270; www.budget.co.nz; 163 Beach Rd; ☺ 8am-5pm)

Escape (☑ 0800 216 171; www.escaperentals.co.nz; 61 The Strand; ☺ 9am-3pm) Eccentrically painted campervans.

Gateway 2 NZ (☑ 0508 225 587; www.gateway2nz.co.nz; 50 Ascot Rd, Mangere; ☺ 7am-7pm)

Gateway Motor Home Hire (☑ 09-296 1652; www.motorhomehire.co.nz; 33 Spartan Rd, Takanini)

Go Rentals (☑ 09-257 5142; www.gorentals.co.nz; Bay 4-10, Cargo Central, George Bolt Memorial Dr, Mangere; ☺ 6am-10pm)

Hertz (☑ 09-367 6350; www.hertz.co.nz; 154 Victoria St; ☺ 7.30am-5.30pm)

Jucy (☑ 0800 399 736; www.jucy.co.nz; 2-16 The Strand; ☺ 8am-5pm)

Kea, Maui & Britz (☑ 09-255 3910; www.maui.co.nz; 36 Richard Pearse Dr, Mangere; ☺ 8am-6pm)

NZ Frontiers (☑ 09-299 6705; www.newzealandfrontiers.com; 30 Laurie Ave, Papakura)

View from Mt Eden (p59)

Omega (☑ 09-377 5573; www.omegarentals. com; 75 Beach Rd; ⊗ 8am-5pm)

Quality (☑ 0800 680 123; www.qualityrental. co.nz; 8 Andrew Baxter Dr, Mangere; ⊗ 8am-4pm)

Thrifty (☑ 09-309 0111; www.thrifty.co.nz; 150 Khyber Pass Rd; ⊗ 8am-5pm)

Wilderness Motorhomes (☑ 09-255 5300; www.wilderness.co.nz; 11 Pavilion Dr, Mangere; ⊗ 8am-5pm)

Purchase

Mechanical inspection services are on hand at secondhand car fairs, where sellers pay to display their cars.

Auckland Car Fair (☑ 09-529 2233; www. carfair.co.nz; Ellerslie Racecourse, Green Lane East; display fee $35; ⊗ 9am-noon Sun) Auckland's largest car fair.

Auckland City Car Fair (☑ 09-837 7817; www. aucklandcitycarfair.co.nz; 6 West St; display fee $30; ⊗ 8am-3pm Sat)

MOTORCYCLE

NZ Motorcycle Rentals (☑ 09-486 2472; www. nzbike.com; 72 Barrys Point Rd, Takapuna; per day $140-290) Guided tours of NZ also available.

ℹ Getting Around

CAR & MOTORCYCLE

Auckland's motorways jam badly at peak times, particularly the Northern and Southern Motorways. It's best to avoid them between 7am and 9am, and from 4pm to 7pm. Things also get tight during term time around 3pm, which is the end of the school day.

Expect to pay for parking in the central Auckland area from 8am to 10pm. Most parking meters operate on a pay-and-display basis and take coins and credit cards; display tickets inside your windscreen. City fringe parking is free on Sundays.

Prices can be steep at parking buildings. Better value are the council-run open-air car parks near the old train station at 126 Beach Rd ($8 per day) and on Ngaoho Pl, off the Strand ($7 per day).

PUBLIC TRANSPORT

The **Auckland Transport** (☑ 09-366 6400; www.at.govt.nz) information service covers buses, trains and ferries, and has an excellent trip-planning feature.

Auckland's public transport system is run by a hodgepodge of different operators, but there is now an integrated AT HOP smartcard (www. athop.co.nz), which provides discounts of at least 20% on most buses, trains and ferries. AT HOP cards cost $10 (nonrefundable), so are really only worthwhile if you're planning an extended stay in Auckland. An AT HOP day pass costs $16 and provides a day's transport on most trains and buses and on North Shore ferries.

Ferry

Auckland's Edwardian baroque **Ferry Building** (99 Quay St) sits grandly at the end of Queen St. Ferry services run by **Fullers** (☑ 09-367 9111; www.fullers.co.nz; to Bayswater, Birkenhead, Devonport, Great Barrier Island, Half Moon Bay, Northcote Point, Motuihe, Motutapu, Rangitoto and Waiheke), **360 Discovery** (☑ 09-307 8005; www.fullers.co.nz; to Coromandel, Gulf Harbour, Motuihe, Rotoroa and Tiritiri Matangi) and **Explore** (☑ 0800 000 469; www.explorewaiheke.co.nz; to Motutapu, Rangitoto and Waiheke) leave from adjacent piers.

Sealink (☑ 0800 732 546; www.sealink. co.nz) ferries to Great Barrier Island leave from Wynyard Wharf, along with some car ferries to Waiheke, but most of the Waiheke car ferries leave from Half Moon Bay in east Auckland.

AROUND AUCKLAND

Piha

If you notice an Auckland surfer dude with a faraway look, chances are they're daydreaming about Piha. This beautiful iron-sand beach has long been a favourite for Aucklanders escaping from the city's stresses.

Piha may be bigger and more populated than neighbouring Karekare, but there's still no supermarket, liquor shop, bank or petrol station, although there is a small general store that doubles as a cafe, takeaway shop and post office.

Sights & Activities

The view of the coast as you drive down Piha Rd is spectacular. Along the beach, the waves crash through the Gap and form a safe swimming hole. A small colony of little penguins nests at the beach's north end.

For surfboard hire, try Piha Store or Piha Surf Shop (p70).

Sleeping & Eating

★ **Piha Beachstay –
Jandal Palace**   HOSTEL **$**
(☑ 09-812 8381; www.pihabeachstay.co.nz; 38 Glenesk Rd; dm/s $35/70, d $120, without bathroom $80; @ 🛜) Attractive and ecofriendly, this wood-and-glass lodge has extremely smart facilities. It's 1km from the beach but there's a little stream at the bottom of the property and bush walks nearby. In winter an open fire warms the large communal lounge.

Piha Surf Accommodation   CABIN **$**
(☑ 09-812 8723; www.pihasurf.co.nz; 122 Seaview Rd; caravans & cabins $60-90) Each basic but charmingly tatty caravan has its own linen, TV, fridge, cooker and long-drop toilet,

and they share a very simple shower. The private cabins have the same rudimentary bathroom arrangement but are a more comfortable option.

Black Sands Lodge   APARTMENT **$$**
(☑ 021 969 924; www.pihabeach.co.nz; Beach Valley Rd; cabin $160, apt $220-260; 🛜) These two modern conjoined apartments with private decks match their prime location with appealing touches, such as stereos and DVD players. The cabin is kitted out in a 1950s Kiwiana bach style and shares a bathroom with the main house. Bikes and wi-fi are free for guests, and in-room massage and lavish dinners can be arranged on request.

Piha Store   BAKERY **$**
(☑ 09-812 8844; 26 Seaview Rd; snacks $2-10; ⊙ 7.30am-5.30pm) Call in for pies and other baked goods, groceries and ice creams. The attached Lion Rock Surf Shop rents surfboards and body boards.

Piha Cafe   CAFE **$$**
(☑ 09-812 8808; www.pihacafe.com; 20 Seaview Rd; mains $14-27; ⊙ 8.30am-3.30pm Mon-Wed, to 10pm Thu-Sat, to 5pm Sun) 🌿 Big-city standards mesh seamlessly with sand-between-toes informality at this attractive, ecofriendly cafe. Cooked breakfasts and crispy pizzas provide sustenance for a hard day's surfing. After the waves, head back for a cold beverage on the deck.

Piha Beach

Shopping

Piha Surf Shop   OUTDOOR EQUIPMENT
(☑ 09-812 8723; www.pihasurf.co.nz; 122 Seaview
Rd; ☺ 8am-5pm) A family-run venture, with
well-known surfboard designer Mike Jolly
selling his wares and wife Pam selling a
small range of crafts. Surfboards (per three
hours/day $25/35), wetsuits ($8/15) and
body boards ($15/25) can be hired, and pri-
vate surfing lessons can be arranged.

West Coast Gallery   ARTS, CRAFTS
(☑ 09-812 8029; www.westcoastgallery.co.nz; Seaview Rd; ☺ 10am-5pm) The work of more than
200 local artists is sold from this small not-
for-profit gallery next to the Piha fire station.

Te Henga (Bethells Beach)

Bethells Beach is reached by taking Te Henga Rd at the northern end of Scenic Dr.

Eating

Bethells Cafe   BURGERS, PIZZA $
(☑ 09-810 9387; www.facebook.com/thebethellscafe;
beach car park; mains $12-17; ☺ 5.30-9.30pm Fri,
10am-6pm Sat & Sun Nov-May, 10am-6pm Sun Jun-
Oct) Less a cafe and more a food truck with
an awning, the Bethells Cafe does a roaring

trade in burgers (beef and vegetarian), pizza,
cakes and coffee. On Friday nights it's pretty much the perfect Kiwi beach scene, with
live musicians entertaining the adults while
the kids surf the sand dunes. Enquire about
glamping opportunities nearby.

Kumeu & Around

Activities

Kumeu River   WINERY
(☑ 09-412 8415; www.kumeuriver.co.nz; 550
SH16; ☺ 9am-4.30pm Mon-Fri, 11am-4.30pm Sat)
Owned by the Brajkovich family, this winery produces one of NZ's best chardonnays,
among other varietals.

Coopers Creek   WINERY
(☑ 09-412 8560; www.cooperscreek.co.nz; 601
SH16, Huapai; ☺ 10.30am-5.30pm) Buy a bottle,
spread out a picnic in the attractive gardens
and, from January to Easter, enjoy Sunday
afternoon jazz sessions.

Eating & Drinking

Tasting Shed   TAPAS $$
(☑ 09-412 6454; www.thetastingshed.co.nz; 609
SH16, Huapai; dishes $14-26; ☺ 4-10pm Wed & Thu,

Vineyards, Kumeu region

noon-11pm Fri-Sun) Complementing its rural aspect with rustic chic decor, this slick eatery conjures up delicious dishes designed to be shared. It's not strictly tapas, as the menu strays from Spain, and appropriates flavours from Asia, the Middle East, Croatia, Serbia, Italy and France.

Hallertau BREWERY
(☑ 09-412 5555; www.hallertau.co.nz; 1171 Coatesville-Riverhead Hwy, Riverhead; ⊙ 11am-midnight) Hallertau offers tasting paddles ($14) of its craft beers served on a vine-covered terrace edging the restaurant. Regular guest beers, good food (shared plates $11 to $15, mains $24 to $31), and occasional weekend DJs and live music make it very popular with Auckland's hopheads.

Riverhead PUB
(☑ 09-412 8902; www.theriverhead.co.nz; cnr Queen & York Sts, Riverhead; ⊙ 11am-late) A blissful terrace, shaded by oak trees and overlooking the river, makes this 1857 hotel a memorable drink stop, even if the menu (mains $26 to $36) doesn't quite live up to its gastropub ambitions. Make a day of it, with a boat cruise from the city to the pub's own jetty.

Helensville

A smattering of heritage buildings, antique shops and cafes makes village-like Helensville a good whistle-stop for those taking SH16 north.

🏃 Activities

Tree Adventures OUTDOORS
See p35

Woodhill Mountain Bike Park MOUNTAIN BIKING
See p35

Parakai Springs SWIMMING, SPA
See p35

ℹ️ Information

Visitor Information Centre (☑ 09-420 8060; www.helensville.co.nz; 5 Commercial Rd; ⊙ 10am-4pm Mon-Sat) Housed inside the Art Stop Cafe. Pick up free brochures detailing the *Helensville Heritage Trail* and *Helensville Riverside Walkway*.

Puhoi

🔵 Sights & Activities

Bohemian Museum MUSEUM
See p33

Church of Sts Peter & Paul CHURCH
(www.holyname.org.nz; Puhoi Rd) The village's pretty Catholic church dates from 1881 and has an interesting tabernacle painting (a copy of one in Bohemia), stained glass and statues.

Puhoi River Canoe Hire CANOEING, KAYAKING
See p33

🍴 Eating & Drinking

Puhoi Valley CAFE **$$**
(☑ 09-422 0670; www.puhoivalley.co.nz; 275 Ahuroa Rd; mains $15-22; ⊙ 10am-4pm) Renowned across NZ, Puhoi Valley cheese features heavily on the menu of this upmarket cheese shop and cafe, set blissfully alongside a lake, fountain and children's playground. In the summer there's music on the lawn, perfect with a gourmet ice cream.

★**Puhoi Pub** PUB
(☑ 09-422 0812; www.puhoipub.com; 5 Saleyards Rd; ⊙ 10am-10pm Mon-Sat, to 8pm Sun) There's character and then some in this 1879 pub, with walls completely covered in old photos, animal heads and vintage household goods.

Gannet among decoys in Tawharanui Regional Park (p34)

Matakana

👁 Sights & Activities

Tawharanui Regional Park BEACH
See p34

Omaha Beach BEACH
The nearest swimming beach to Matakana, Omaha has a long stretch of white sand, good surf and ritzy holiday homes.

Blue Adventures WATER SPORTS
(☑ 022 630 5705; www.blueadventures.co.nz; 331 Omaha Flats Rd, Omaha; lessons per hr $40-80) Offers kitesurfing, paddle boarding and wakeboarding lessons from Omaha and Orewa.

Matakana Bicycle Hire BICYCLE RENTAL
(☑ 09-423 0076; www.matakanabicyclehire.co.nz; 951 Matakana Rd; half-/full-day hire from $30/40, tours from $70) Hire a bike to explore local vineyards and beaches.

🍴 Eating & Drinking

Mahurangi River
Winery & Restaurant MODERN NZ $$
(☑ 09-425 0306; www.mahurangiriver.co.nz; 162 Hamilton Rd; mains $28-34; ☺ 11am-4pm Thu-Mon) Expansive vineyard views partner with a relaxed ambience and savvy food at this rural spot off Sandspit Rd.

The Matakana PUB FOOD $$
(☑ 09-422 7518; www.matakana.co.nz; 11 Matakana Valley Rd; mains $17-25; ☺ noon-12.30am) Following a trendy makeover, Matakana's heritage pub now features quirky decor, Matakana wines and craft beers, and decent bistro food including local Mahurangi oysters. Occasional DJs and live acts enliven the cool outdoor space.

Vintry WINE BAR
(☑ 09-423 0251; www.thevintry.co.nz; 2 Matakana Valley Rd; ☺ 10am-10pm) In the Matakana Cinemas complex, this wine bar serves as a one-stop cellar door for all the local producers.

ℹ Information

Matakana Information Centre (☑ 09-422 7433; www.matakanainfo.org.nz; 2 Matakana Valley Rd; ☺ 10am-1pm) In the foyer of the Matakana Cinemas complex.

Goat Island Marine Reserve

There are dive areas all around Goat Island, which sits just offshore, or you can snorkel or dive directly from the beach. Colourful sponges, forests of seaweed, boarfish, crayfish and stingrays are common sights, and if you're very lucky you may see orcas and bottle-nosed dolphins. Visibility is claimed to be at least 10m, 75% of the time.

⊙ Sights & Activities

Goat Island

Marine Discovery Centre AQUARIUM

(☑ 09-923 3645; www.goatislandmarine.co.nz; 160 Goat Island Rd, Leigh; adult/child/family $9/7/20; ⊙ 10am-4pm daily Dec-Feb, Sat & Sun Mar-Nov) Staffed by marine experts and graduate students from the University of Auckland, this centre is packed with interesting exhibitions on the ecosystem of the marine reserve, and is worth visiting before venturing into Goat Island's waters. The interactive displays and the tide pool full of marine creatures are great for children.

Octopus Hideaway SNORKELLING

(☑ 09-422 6212; www.theoctopushideaway.nz; 7 Goat Island Rd; ⊙ 10am-5pm) Up the road from the beach, this crew hires snorkelling gear (adult/child $25/18, including wetsuit $38/26), and offers guided two-hour day ($75/55) and night ($95/70) snorkel expeditions.

Goat Island Dive & Snorkel DIVING

(☑ 09-422 6925; www.goatislanddive.co.nz; 142a Pakiri Rd; snorkel set hire adult/child $25/18, incl wetsuit $38/26) This long-standing operator offers guided snorkelling, PADI courses and dive trips in the Goat Island Marine Reserve and other key sites throughout the year. It also hires snorkelling and diving gear.

☞ Tours

Glass Bottom Boat Tours BOAT TOUR

(☑ 09-422 6334; www.glassbottomboat.co.nz; Goat Island Rd; adult/child $28/15) A glass-bottomed boat provides an opportunity to see the underwater life while staying dry. Trips last 45 minutes and run from the beach year-round, weather permitting; go online or ring to check conditions and to book. It also hires snorkel sets (per two/four hours $28/36), kayaks (per hour $28) and offers guided snorkelling for beginners (adult/child $75/55).

🍷 Drinking & Nightlife

Leigh Sawmill Cafe PUB

(☑ 09-422 6019; www.sawmillcafe.co.nz; 142 Pakiri Rd; ⊙ 10am-late daily Jan-Mar, 10am-late Thu-Sun Apr-Nov) This spunky little venue is a regular stop on the summer rock circuit, sometimes attracting surprisingly big names. The pizzas ($14 to $35) are thin and crunchy like they should be, and best enjoyed in the garden on a lazy summer's evening.

Waiheke Island

While beaches are Waiheke's biggest drawcard, wine is a close second. There are around 30 boutique wineries scattered about, many with tasting rooms, swanky restaurants and breathtaking views. The island also boasts plenty of quirky galleries and craft stores, a lasting legacy of its hippyish past.

When you've had enough of supping, dining, lazing on the sand and splashing in the surf, there are plenty of other pursuits to engage in. A network of walking trails leads through nature reserves and past the cliff-top holiday homes of the Auckland elite. The kayaking is excellent and there are ziplines to whiz along and clay pigeons to shoot. All in all, it's a magical place.

⊙ Sights

Beaches

Waiheke's two best beaches are Onetangi, a long stretch of white sand at the centre of the island, and Palm Beach, a pretty little horseshoe bay between Oneroa and Onetangi. Both have nudist sections; head west just past some rocks in both cases. Oneroa and neighbouring Little Oneroa are also excellent, but you'll be sharing the waters with moored yachts in summer. Reached by an unsealed road through farmland, Man O' War Bay is a compact sheltered beach that's excellent for swimming.

Wineries

Goldie Wines WINERY

(☑ 09-372 7493; www.goldiewines.co.nz; 18 Causeway Rd, Surfdale; tastings $10, refundable with purchase; ⊙ noon-4pm) Founded as Goldwater Estate in 1978, this is Waiheke's pioneering vineyard. The attached delicatessen sells well-stocked baskets for a picnic among the vines ($55 for two people).

Man O' War WINERY

(☑ 09-372 9678; www.manowarvineyards.co.nz; 725 Man O' War Bay Rd; ⊙ 11am-6pm Dec-Feb, to 4.30pm Mar-Nov) Settle in with a tapas platter and a glass of Man O' War's Valhalla Chardonnay at Waiheke's only beachfront tasting room. If the weather is good, go for a swim in beautiful Man O' War Bay.

Passage Rock Wines WINERY

(☑ 09-372 7257; www.passagerockwines.co.nz; 438 Orapiu Rd; ⊙ 11am-4pm daily Jan, Wed-Sun Feb-Apr & Dec, Sat & Sun Aug-Nov) 'Waiheke's

Waiheke Island

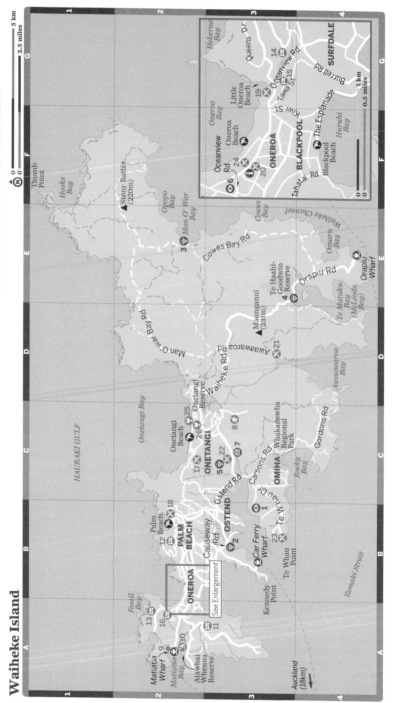

HAURAKI GULF

Thumb
Point

Hooks
Bay

Stony Batter
(220m)▲

Opopo
Bay

Man O' War
Bay

3🏛

Cowes
Bay

Cowes Bay Rd

Waiheke Channel

Te Haahi-
Goodwin
Reserve

4🏛

Orapiu Rd

Omaru
Bay

Orapiu
Wharf

E🏛

Te Matuku
Bay
(McLeods
Bay)

Awaawaroa Rd

Maunganui
(231m)▲

21🏛

Man O' War Bay Rd

Waiheke Rd

Onetangi
Reserve

Onetangi Bay

25🏛
26🏛

Onetangi
Beach

ONETANGI

17🏛
5🏛 22🏛
8🏛
7🏛

Ostend Rd

OSTEND

Carsons Rd

OMIHA

Whakanewha
Regional
Park

Rocky
Bay

Gordons Rd

Awaawaroa
Bay

Palm
Beach

18🏛
12🏛

PALM
BEACH

Causeway
Rd

Fossil
Bay

13🏛
16🏛

ONEROA

See Enlargement

11🏛

Matiatia
Wharf

9🏛

Atawhai
Whenua
Reserve

Matiatia
Bay

10🏛

2🏛

Car Ferry
Wharf

Kennedy
Point

Te Whau
Point

1🏛

23🏛

Te Whau Dr

Tamaki Strait

Auckland
(18km)

Enlargement (inset)

SURFDALE

Hekerua
Bay

Queens Dr

Oneroa
Bay

14🏛

Oceanview Rd

15🏛

Tawa St

19🏛

Little
Oneroa
Beach

Burrell Rd

Kiwi St

Oceanview
Rd

24🏛

ONEROA

Oneroa
Beach

6🏛

20🏛

The Esplanade

Huruhi
Bay

BLACKPOOL

Blackpool
Beach

Tahatai Rd

Blackpool
Rd

0   1 km
0   0.5 miles

N

0   5 km
0   2.5 miles

Waiheke Island

most awarded winery' serves excellent pizza among the vines.

Stonyridge   WINERY
See p52

Wild On Waiheke   WINERY, BREWERY
See p52

Art, History & Culture

The *Waiheke Art Map* brochure, free from the i-SITE (p79) lists galleries and craft stores.

Dead Dog Bay   GARDENS
(☑ 09-372 6748; www.deaddogbay.co.nz; 100 Margaret Reeve Lane; adult/child $10/free; ⊙ 9am-5pm) Wander steep pathways through privately owned rainforest, wetlands and gardens scattered with sculpture.

Waiheke Island Artworks   ARTS CENTRE
(2 Korora Rd, Oneroa) The Artworks complex houses the **Artworks Theatre** (☑ 09-372 2941; www.artworkstheatre.org.nz), the **Waiheke Island Community Cinema** (☑ 09-372 4240; www.waihekecinema.net; adult/child $15/8), the attention-grabbing **Waiheke Community Art Gallery** (☑ 09-372 9907; www.waihekeartgallery.org.nz; ⊙ 10am-4pm) FREE and **Whittaker's Musical Museum** (☑ 09-372 5573; www.musical-museum.org; suggested donation $5; ⊙ 1-4pm, live shows 1.30pm Sat), a collection of antique instruments. This is also the place for free internet access, either on a terminal at the **Waiheke Library** (☑ 09-374 1325; www.aucklandlibraries.govt.nz; ⊙ 9am-6pm Mon-Fri, 10.30am-4pm Sat; ☎) or on its wi-fi network.

Waiheke Museum & Historic Village   MUSEUM
(www.waihekemuseum.org.nz; 165 Onetangi Rd; admission by donation; ⊙ noon-4pm Wed, Sat & Sun) Displays islander artefacts in six restored buildings.

Activities

Tramping

Ask at the i-SITE about the island's beautiful coastal walks (ranging from one to three hours) and the 3km **Cross Island Walkway** (from Onetangi to Rocky Bay). Other tracks traverse **Whakanewha Regional Park**, a haven for rare coastal birds and geckos, and the Royal Forest & Bird Protection Society's three reserves: **Onetangi** (Waiheke Rd), **Te Haahi-Goodwin** (Orapiu Rd) and **Atawhai Whenua** (Ocean View Rd).

Other Activities

EcoZip Adventures   ZIPLINING
See p54

Ross Adventures   KAYAKING
(☑ 09-372 5550; www.kayakwaiheke.co.nz; Matiatia Beach; half-/full-day trips $125/195, per 1/2/3/6hr $30/45/50/60) It's the fervently held opinion of Ross that Waiheke offers kayaking every bit as good as the legendary Abel Tasman National Park. He should know – he's been offering guided kayak trips for over 20 years. Experienced sea kayakers can comfortably circumnavigate the island in four days, exploring hidden coves and sand spits inaccessible by land.

👆 Tours

Ananda Tours TOUR
(☑ 09-372 7530; www.ananda.co.nz) Wine tours ($110), gourmet wine and food tours ($170), and a wine connoisseurs' tour ($250) are among the options. Small-group, informal tours can be customised, including visits to artists' studios.

Waiheke Island Wine Tours TOUR
(☑ 09-372 2140; www.waihekeislandwinetours. co.nz) Options include Views, Vines & Wines ($110 per person, six hours with a two-hour break for lunch at a restaurant of your choice), tailor-made Platinum Private Tours ($495 per couple) and Indulgence Two-Day Tours ($920 per person including two nights' accommodation).

Hike Bike Ako WALKING, CYCLING
(☑ 021 465 373; www.hikebikeako.co.nz; tour 3/5hr $99/125) Explore the island with Māori guides on a walking or biking tour, or a combination of both. Tours include pick-up from the ferry, and a large dose of Māori legend, history and culture.

Potiki Adventures CULTURAL TOUR
(☑ 021 422 773; www.potikiadventures.co.nz; adult/child from $150/80) Day-long island tours from a Māori cultural perspective, including beaches, a bush walk, a vineyard visit and demonstrations of traditional musical instruments and weaving.

Fullers TOUR
(☑ 09-367 9111; www.fullers.co.nz) Runs a Wine on Waiheke tour (adult $130, 4½ hours, departs Auckland 1pm) visiting three of the island's top wineries, and including a platter of nibbles; Taste of Waiheke (adult $140, 5½ hours, departs Auckland 11am) includes three wineries plus an olive grove and light lunch. There's also a 1½-hour Explorer Tour (adult/child $57/29, departs Auckland 10am, 11am and noon).

Other packages include EcoZip's zipline, and car hire. All prices include the ferry and an all-day local bus pass.

🎊 Festivals & Events

Headland Sculpture on the Gulf ART
(www.sculptureonthegulf.co.nz; ⊙ Feb) A 2.5km cliff-top sculpture walk, held for a month in February in odd-numbered years.

Waiheke Island of Wine Vintage Festival WINE, FOOD
(www.waihekevintagefestival.co.nz; ⊙ mid-Mar) Five days of wine, food and music events. Seventeen different vineyards are involved, and shuttle buses travel between the various locations.

Waiheke Island International Jazz Festival MUSIC
(www.waihekejazzfestival.co.nz; prices vary by event; ⊙ Mar/Apr) Local and international acts across the island from Friday to Sunday during Easter.

🛏 Sleeping

Waiheke is so popular in the summer holidays that many locals rent out their houses and bugger off elsewhere. You'll need to book ahead and even then there are very few bargains. Prices drop considerably in winter, especially midweek. For midrange accommodation, a good option is to book a holiday home through www.bookabach.co.nz or www.holidayhouses.co.nz.

Boating around coastline of Waiheke Island
CULTURA TRAVEL/LAURA ARSIE/GETTY IMAGES ©

Vineyards, Waiheke Island

★ **Fossil Bay Lodge**   CABIN **$**

(☑ 09-372 8371; www.fossilbay.net; 58 Korora Rd, Oneroa; s $60, d $85-90, tents $100-120, apt $130; 🛜) Three cutesy cabins open onto a courtyard facing the main building, which houses the communal toilets, kitchen and living area, and a compact self-contained upstairs apartment. Best of all are the four 'glamping' tents, each with a proper bed and its own toilet. Apart from the occasional squawking duck – or toddler from the adjacent Steiner kindergarten – it's a peaceful place.

Hekerua Lodge   HOSTEL **$**

(☑ 09-372 8990; www.hekerualodge.co.nz; 11 Hekerua Rd, Oneroa; sites $18, dm $31-33, s $55, d $90-120; 🛜💦) This secluded hostel is surrounded by native bush and has a barbecue, stone-tiled pool, spa pool, sunny deck, casual lounge area and its own walking track. It's far from luxurious, but it has a laid-back and social feel.

Tawa Lodge   GUESTHOUSE **$$**

(☑ 09-372 6675; www.pungalodge.co.nz; 15 Tawa St, Oneroa; r $110-120, apt $175-225; 🛜) Between the self-contained two-person cottage at the front (our pick of the lot, due to the sublimely romantic views) and the apartment and house at the rear are three reasonably priced loft rooms sharing a small kitchen and bathroom.

★ **Enclosure Bay**   B&B **$$$**

(☑ 09-372 8882; www.enclosurebay.co.nz; 9 Great Barrier Rd; r/ste $390/495; 🛜) If you're going to shell out for a luxury B&B you expect it to be special, and that's certainly what's offered here. Each of the three guest rooms has sumptuous views and balconies, and the owners subscribe to the nothing's-too-much-trouble school of hospitality.

Waiheke Dreams   RENTAL HOUSE **$$$**

(☑ 09-818 7129; www.waihekedreams.co.nz; 43 Tiri Rd, Oneroa; 1-/2-bedroom house $200/300) Dream a little dream of a luxurious, modern, spacious, open-plan, two-bedroom house on the crest of a hill with unsurpassed views over Oneroa Bay and the Hauraki Gulf – then pinch yourself and wake up with a smug smile in View43. Tucked at the rear is the considerably smaller one-bedroom CityLights, which glimpses Auckland's glimmer over the back lawn.

Cable Bay Views   APARTMENT **$$$**

(☑ 09-372 2901; www.cablebayviews.co.nz; 103 Church Bay Rd; r $300; 🛜) These three modern, self-contained studio apartments have stellar vineyard views and are handy to a couple of Waiheke's best vineyard restaurants. Check the website for good midweek and off-peak discounts.

✕ Eating

Waiheke has some excellent eateries and, if you're lucky, the views will be enough to distract from the hole being bored into your hip pocket. There's a supermarket in Ostend.

Dragonfired
PIZZA $

(☑ 021 922 289; www.dragonfired.co.nz; Little Oneroa Beach, Oneroa; mains $10-18; ⊗10am-8pm daily Dec-Feb, 11am-7pm Fri-Sun Mar-Nov; 🍴) Specialising in 'artisan woodfired food', this caravan by the beach serves the three Ps: pizza, polenta plates and pocket bread. It's easily Waiheke's best place for cheap eats. It has another location by the shop in **Palm Beach** (☑ 0272 372 372; Matapana Reserve, Palm Beach; ⊗10am-8pm daily Dec-Feb, 11am-7pm Fri-Sun Mar-Nov).

Shed at Te Motu
MODERN NZ $$

(☑ 09-372 6884; www.temotu.co.nz/the-shed; 76 Onetangi Rd; shared plates small $12-18, large $22-36; ⊗noon-3pm daily, 6pm-late Fri & Sat Nov-Apr, reduced hours in winter) Shared plates featuring global flavours are served by the restaurant's savvy and equally international wait staff. Highlights include shiitake pancakes with kimchi and black garlic, or the wonderfully slow-cooked lamb shoulder partnered with a delicate biryani-spiced pilaf. Te Motu's standout wines are its stellar Bordeaux-style blends.

Sculptures of Māori gods, Waiheke Island
TOM ANG/GETTY IMAGES ©

On Friday nights, the Shed offers a good-value prix-fixe menu (two/three courses $45/55). Bookings are recommended for both lunch and dinner.

Oyster Inn
SEAFOOD $$

(☑ 09-372 2222; www.theoysterinn.co.nz; 124 Oceanview Rd, Oneroa; mains $28-35; ⊗noon-late) The Oyster Inn is a popular destination for Auckland's smart set. They're attracted by the excellent seafood-skewed bistro menu, oysters and champagne, and a buzzy but relaxed vibe that's part bar and part restaurant. In summer, brunch on the veranda is a great way to ease into another Waiheke day.

Casita Miro
SPANISH $$

(☑ 09-372 7854; www.casitamiro.co.nz; 3 Brown St, Onetangi; tapas $12-20, ración $26; ⊗noon-3pm Thu-Mon, 6-10pm Fri & Sat) A wrought-iron and glass pavilion backed with a Gaudí-esque mosaic garden is the stage for a very entertaining troupe of servers who will guide you through the menu of delectable tapas and *ración* (larger dishes), designed to be shared. In summer the sides open up, but otherwise, at busy times, it can get noisy.

Wai Kitchen
CAFE $$

(☑ 09-372 7505; www.waikitchen.co.nz; 1/149 Oceanview Rd, Oneroa; mains $17-26; ⊗8.30am-3.30pm, extended hours in summer; 🍴) Why? Well firstly there's the lively menu that abounds with Mediterranean and Asian flavours. Then there's the charming service and the breezy ambience of this glassed-in wedge, facing the *wai* (water).

Poderi Crisci
ITALIAN $$

(☑ 09-372 2148; www.podericrisci.co.nz; 205 Awaawaroa Rd; lunch mains $25-33, dinner degustation $85; ⊗noon-5pm Sun, Mon & Thu, to 10pm Fri & Sat May-Sep, extended hours Oct-Apr) 🍴 Poderi Crisci has quickly gained a sterling reputation for its food, particularly its legendary four-hour lunches on Sundays ($70 per person). Italian varietals and olives have been planted alongside the existing vines, and tastings are offered in the atmospheric cellar ($10, refunded upon purchase). It's definitely worth the drive into the winery's isolated valley, but book first.

Cable Bay
MODERN NZ $$$

(☑ 09-372 5889; www.cablebay.co.nz; 12 Nick Johnstone Dr; mains $42-44; ⊗noon-3pm Tue-Sun, 6pm-late Tue-Sat; 🛜) Impressive uber-modern architecture, interesting sculpture and beautiful views set the scene for this acclaimed restaurant. The food is sublime, but if your budget won't stretch to a meal, stop in for a wine tasting ($10 for five wines, refundable with a purchase, 11am to 5pm daily) or platters and shared plates at the Verandah bar.

Te Whau   MODERN NZ **$$$**
See p54

🍷 Drinking & Nightlife

Sand Shack   BAR, CAFE
(☑ 09-372 2565; www.fourthavenue.co.nz; 1 Fourth Ave, Onetangi; ⊙ 8am-11pm) Part bar and part beach cafe, all served up with cool decor and Onetangi Beach views from the sunny deck. There's a good selection of tap beers and a menu of uncomplicated stomach fillers such as cooked breakfasts, burgers and pizzas.

Charlie Farley's   BAR
(☑ 09-372 4106; www.charliefarleys.co.nz; 21 The Strand, Onetangi; ⊙ 8.30am-late) It's easy to see why the locals love this place when you're supping on a Waiheke wine or beer under the pohutukawa on the beach-gazing deck.

ℹ️ Information

Waiheke Island i-SITE (☑ 09-372 1234; www.aucklandnz.com; 116 Ocean View Rd; ⊙ 9am-4pm) As well as the very helpful main office, there's a (usually unstaffed) counter in the ferry terminal at Matiatia Wharf.

ℹ️ Getting Around

BICYCLE
Various bicycle routes are outlined in the *Bike Waiheke!* brochure, available from the wharf and the i-SITE; be prepared for a few hills.

Waiheke Bike Hire (☑ 09-372 7937; www.waihekebikehire.co.nz; Matiatia; per day $35) hires mountain bikes from its base in the car park near the wharf.

Parts of Waiheke are quite hilly, so ease the load with a hybrid machine from **Onya Bikes** (☑ 022 050 2233; www.ecyclesnz.com; 124 Oceanview Rd; per hr/day $20/60), combining pedalling with electric motors.

CAR, MOTORCYCLE & SCOOTER
There are petrol stations in Oneroa and Onetangi.
Fun Rentals (☑ 09-372 8001; www.funrentals.co.nz; 14a Belgium St, Ostend; per day car/scooter/4WD from $59/49/59) Includes free pick-ups and drop-offs to the ferries.

Rent Me Waiheke (☑ 09-372 3339; www.rentmewaiheke.co.nz; 14 Oceanview Rd, Matiatia; per day car/scooter $69/59)

Waiheke Auto Rentals (☑ 09-372 8998; www.waihekerentals.co.nz; Matiatia Wharf; per day car/scooter from $79/69)

Waiheke Rental Cars (☑ 09-372 8635; www.waihekerentalcars.co.nz; Matiatia Wharf; per day car/4WD from $79/109)

STRETCH YOUR LEGS
AUCKLAND

Start/Finish: Sky Tower

Distance: 5km

Duration: Three hours

Ascend the soaring Sky Tower for stunning views of Auckland's impetuous sprawl across two harbours, before discovering iconic New Zealand art, the city's proud maritime history, and emerging areas for great eating, drinking and shopping.

Take this walk on Trips

Sky Tower

At 328m, Auckland's Sky Tower (p59) is the southern hemisphere's tallest structure, and a lift reaches the observation decks in 40 stomach-lurching seconds. There's underground parking here, and adjacent Federal St is packed with excellent restaurants.

The Walk » Walk along Federal St and turn left down Wellesley St to the Civic Theatre.

Civic Theatre

The Civic Theatre (📞09-309 2677; www. civictheatre.co.nz; cnr Queen & Wellesley Sts), built in 1929, is one of only seven 'atmospheric theatres' remaining in the world, and a fine survivor from cinema's Golden Age. The auditorium features lavish Moorish decoration, and the stunning foyer is an Indian confection with elephants and monkeys hanging from every conceivable fixture.

The Walk » Cross Queen St and walk up Wellesley St before turning left into Kitchener St for the Auckland Art Gallery.

Auckland Art Gallery

Combining a modern glass-and-wood atrium with an 1887 French-chateau frame, the Auckland Art Gallery (p58) features the best of NZ art, along with important works by Picasso, Cézanne, Gauguin and Matisse. Highlights include the intimate, 19th-century portraits of tattooed Māori subjects by Charles Goldie, and the dramatic text-scrawled canvasses of Colin McCahon. Free tours at 11.30am and 1.30pm.

The Walk » Turn right along Lorne St, which becomes High St and continues via Commerce St across Customs St to the Britomart Precinct.

Britomart Precinct

The Britomart Precinct is a compact enclave of historic buildings that has been transformed into one of the city's best eating, drinking and shopping precincts. Most of Auckland's top fashion designers have recently decamped to the Britomart area from further uptown in High St.

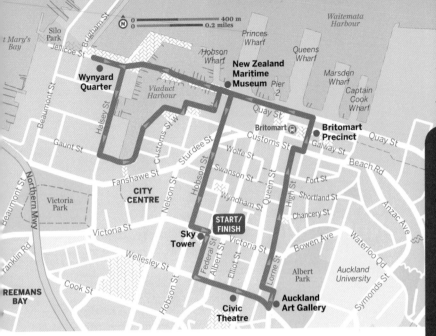

The Walk »
From the Britomart Precinct, walk along Quay St past Auckland's historic Ferry Building to the New Zealand Maritime Museum.

New Zealand Maritime Museum

This museum (☏09-373 0800; www.maritimemuseum.co.nz; 149-159 Quay St; adult/child $20/10, incl harbour cruise $50/25; ⏰9am-5pm, free tours 10.30am & 1pm Mon-Fri) traces NZ's seafaring history from Māori voyaging canoes to America's Cup yachting. Recreations include a 19th-century steerage-class cabin and a 1950s Kiwi bach (holiday home). The exhibit 'Blue Water Black Magic' is a tribute to Sir Peter Blake, the renowned and respected NZ yachtsman who was murdered in 2001 on an environmental monitoring trip in the Amazon.

The Walk » Continue past super yachts to the Wynyard Quarter. Te Wero Bridge is raised when boats need to access the inner harbour.

Wynyard Quarter

Wynyard Quarter opened in advance of 2011's Rugby World Cup, and with its public plazas, waterfront eateries and children's playground, it is a popular place for Aucklanders to gather. At the Silo Park area, down the western end, free outdoor Friday-night **movies** and weekend **markets** are summertime institutions. Most of Wynyard's better restaurants are one block back from the water on Jellicoe Street.

The Walk » Leave the Wynyard Quarter on Halsey St and turn left onto Gaunt St to follow a pedestrian walkway around the marina to Viaduct Harbour (1.4km).

Viaduct Harbour

Once a busy commercial port, Viaduct Harbour was given a major makeover for the 1999/2000 and 2003 America's Cup yachting events. It's now a fancy dining precinct, and guaranteed to have at least a slight buzz any night of the week. Historical plaques, public sculpture and a line-up of millionaires' yachts make it a diverting place for a stroll.

The Walk » Follow Hobson St uphill for 700m to the Sky Tower.

Bay of Islands & Northland

For many New Zealanders, the phrase 'up north' conjures up sepia-toned images of family fun in the sun, pohutukawa in bloom and dolphins frolicking in pretty bays. The site of the earliest settlements of both Māori and Europeans, Northland is unquestionably the birthplace of the nation.

WHANGAREI DISTRICT

Mangawhai

◉ Sights

Mangawhai Heads   BEACH
Across the water from the harbour's south head sits the holiday town with a surf beach at its northern tip. Lifesavers patrol on weekends in summer and daily during school holidays, but it's not especially dangerous.

Mangawhai Museum   MUSEUM
(☑ 09-431 4645; www.mangawhai-museum.org.nz; Molesworth Dr; adult/child $12/3; ⊙10am-4pm) One of regional New Zealand's best museums, this spectacular building on the main road linking Mangawhai village to Mangawhai Heads is packed with interesting displays on the area's history and environment.

Te Whai Bay Wines   VINEYARD
(☑ 09-945 0580; www.tewhaibaywines.co.nz; 26 Bush Lane; ⊙10am-5pm late Oct-Easter, Sat, Sun & public holidays Easter-late Oct) Handcrafted wines include chardonnay, pinot gris and Bordeaux-style red wines, and the beautiful vineyard is a great spot for a shared antipasto platter to enhance the pleasant illusion of being in a southern hemisphere version of Tuscany. Ask at Mangawhai's visitor information centre about other local vineyards.

⚡ Activities

Mangawhai Cliff Top Walkway   TRAMPING
Starting at Mangawhai Heads, this track affords extensive views of sea and land. It takes two to three hours, provided you time it with a return down the beach at low tide. This is part of Te Araroa, the national walking track. Ask at the visitor information centre for the *Tracks and Walks* brochure detailing other walks in the area.

Wined About Bike Tours   BICYCLE TOUR
(☑ 021 945 050, 09-945 0580; www.winedabout. co.nz; per person $50) Three different self-guided tour options include all the good things in life. Art and chocolate, wine and olives, or a freestyle exploration of Mangawhai village and nearby beaches. Pick-ups are included in the prices, both before and after riding.

🛏 Sleeping

Mangawhai Heads Holiday Park   HOLIDAY PARK **$**
(☑ 09-431 4675; www.mangawhaiheadsholiday-park.co.nz; 2 Mangawhai Heads Rd; sites $16-18, units $105-135; 🐾) With an absolute waterfront location on the sandy expanse of Mangawhai's estuary, this laid-back combo of campsites, units and cabins is a retro slice of Kiwiana holiday style. Visit in summer for a vibrant halo of red blooms from groves of pohutukawa trees. Just note it's a family-

friendly place, with an expectation of no noise after 10.30pm.

Sunhill Cottages COTTAGE **$$**
(☑ 09-431 4393; www.sunhill.co.nz; 2306 Cove Rd; cottages $185; 🛜🐾) In rural surroundings just a short inland drive from Mangawhai, Sunhill's two self-contained cottages are spacious and airy, and include private decks looking out to the nearby Brynderwyn ranges. A heated pool and shared outdoor bar area is ideal for relaxing at the end of the day. B&B accommodation (double $130) is also available in the main house.

Mangawhai Lodge B&B **$$$**
(☑ 09-431 5311; www.seaviewlodge.co.nz; 4 Heather St, Mangawhai Heads; s/d $185/190, unit $175-220; 🛜) Smartly furnished rooms have access to a picture-perfect wraparound veranda at this boutique B&B, which also features great views.

✖ Eating & Drinking

Mangawhai Market MARKET **$**
(Moir St; ⊗9am-1pm Sat) Held in the library hall in Mangawhai village, this is a good place to stock up on organic produce (including wine and olive oil) and peruse local crafts. Another market is held on Sunday mornings in the Mangawhai Heads Domain from mid-October to Easter.

★ Wood Street Freehouse CAFE **$$**
(☑ 09-431 4051; www.facebook.com/woodstfreehouse; 12 Wood St, Mangawhai Heads; mains $16-22, shared plates $11-14; ⊗noon-late Mon-Fri, from 10am Sat & Sun) Craft beer has arrived in Mangawhai at this buzzing cafe, including beers from local Northland brewers such as Schippers and the Sawmill Brewery. Excellent food includes burgers, gourmet pizzas and shared plates – the truffle and parmesan fries are addictive – and from Friday to Sunday fresh local oysters from Wood Street's raw bar are best devoured on the sunny deck.

Harvest Blue CAFE **$$**
(☑ 09-431 4111; www.facebook.com/harvestcafe mangawhai; 198 Molesworth Dr; mains $18-28; ⊗8am-2pm Sun, Mon & Thu, to 9pm Fri & Sat) Rustic wooden furniture and overflowing pots of flowers and fresh herbs fill the deck of this relaxed cafe's sunny courtyard. New owners have revitalised the menu, and brunch classics such as Spanish omelette and sweetcorn fritters now segue into Asian-style salads crammed with calamari or tuna

for lunch. On Friday and Saturday, Harvest Blue is also open for dinner.

Evening meals are a good opportunity to try wines from local Mangawhai vineyards Lochiel Estate and Millars.

Mangawhai Tavern PUB
(☑ 09-431 4505; www.mangawhaitavern.co.nz; Moir St; ⊗11am-late) One of the country's oldest pubs – built in 1865 – the tavern's harbourside location is a top spot for an afternoon beer. There's live music most Saturday nights and Sunday afternoons, and across the Christmas–New Year period some of NZ's top bands rock the garden bar. The pub meals are deservedly world-famous-in-Northland.

❶ Information

Visitor Information Centre (☑ 09-431 5090; www.mangawhai.co.nz) Staffed sporadically (mainly on weekends and in summer), but there are information boards outside. Ask about opportunities to visit local vineyards and olive groves.

Waipu

The original 934 British settlers came to Waipu from Scotland via Nova Scotia (Canada) between 1853 and 1860. These dour

Scots had the good sense to eschew frigid Otago, where so many of their kindred settled, for sunnier northern climes. Visit the Waipu Museum (p20) for a glimpse into their story.

There are also excellent walks in the area, including the Waipu Coastal Trail, which heads south from Waipu Cove – around to Langs Beach, passing the Pancake Rocks on the way. The 2km Waipu Caves Walking Track starts at Ormiston Rd and passes through farmland and a scenic reserve en route to a large cave containing glowworms and limestone formations; bring a torch, a compass and sturdy footwear to delve the depths.

🛏 Sleeping & Eating

Waipu Wanderers Backpackers   HOSTEL $
(☏ 09-432 0532; www.waipu-hostel.co.nz; 25 St Marys Rd; dm/s/d $33/50/70; 🛜) There are only three rooms at this friendly backpackers in Waipu township. Look forward to free fruit in season.

Waipu Cove Resort   RESORT, MOTEL $$
(☏ 09-432 0348; www.waipucoveresort.co.nz; 891 Cove Rd; units $120-220; 🛜🏊) Modern self-contained apartments with private courtyards pleasingly blur the line between resort and boutique hotel. Nestled behind sand dunes, the arcing sprawl of the beach is just metres away, and the complex also includes a spa pool and a swimming pool.

Little Red   CAFE $
(www.facebook.com/blackshedwaipu.co.nz; 7 Cove Rd; snacks $4-7; ⊘ 8am-3pm late Oct-Easter) Waipu's best coffee, artisan icy treats, organic soft drinks and kombucha, and homestyle baking – all served from a funky red shipping container. Grab a spot on one of the colourful Cape Cod–style chairs out the front and tuck into brioche and brownies.

Cove Cafe   CAFE $$
(☏ 09-432 0234; 910 Cove Rd, Waipu Cove; breakfast $5-15, pizza $20-24, mains $20-23; ⊘ 7am-10.30pm) This heritage cottage near Waipu covers all the bases, from coffee and breakfast bagels to pizza, gourmet burgers and craft beer, and the deck is a very pleasant spot to celebrate exploring NZ. Healthy smoothies – try the Vita Berry Blast with banana, strawberries and blueberries – will provide a boost for the next stage of your Kiwi itinerary.

McLeod's Pizza Barn   ITALIAN $$
(☏ 09-432 1011; 2 Cove Rd; pizzas $13-28, mains $19-30; ⊘ 11.30am-late Wed-Sun Apr-Nov, daily Dec-Mar) Popular platters, light fare and great pizzas go well with craft beer from Waipu's very own McLeod's Brewery. Partner the Wharfinger pizza with prawns, avocado and feta with the hoppy IPA.

ℹ Information

Tourist brochures and internet access are available at the Waipu Museum.

KIRILL POLISHCHUK/500PX ©

Waipu Caves

Whangarei

⊙ Sights

★ **Whangarei Art Museum**   GALLERY
(☑ 09-430 4240; www.whangareiartmuseum.co.nz; The Hub, Town Basin; admission by donation; ⊙ 10am-4pm) At the Te Manawa Hub information centre (p88), Whangarei's public gallery has an interesting permanent collection, the star of which is a 1904 Māori portrait by Goldie. Also planned is the Hundertwasser Arts Centre, based on architectural plans by the late Austrian artist Friedensreich Hundertwasser. See www.yeswhangarei.co.nz for details of the campaign to raise support and funding for the project.

★ **Clapham's Clocks**   MUSEUM
See p20

Old Library Arts Centre   GALLERY
(☑ 09-430 6432; www.oldlibrary.org.nz; 7 Rust Ave; ⊙ 10am-4pm Tue-Thu) FREE The work of local artists is exhibited in this wonderful art-deco building. Check the website for occasional concerts. Set between the old and new libraries is Pou, an intriguing sculpture consisting of 10 large poles carved with Māori, Polynesian, Celtic, Croatian and Korean motifs. Grab an interpretive pamphlet from the library.

Abbey Caves   CAVE
(Abbey Caves Rd) FREE Abbey Caves is an undeveloped network of three caverns full of glowworms and limestone formations, 6km east of town. Grab a torch, strong shoes, a mate for safety and prepare to get wet. The surrounding reserve is a forest of crazily shaped rock extrusions. Ask at the i-SITE (p88) about an information sheet for the caves.

Whangarei Falls   WATERFALL
(Otuihau; Ngunguru Rd) Short walks around these 26m-high falls provide views of the water cascading over the edge of an old basalt lava flow. The falls can be reached on the Tikipunga bus ($3, no service on Sundays), leaving from Rose St in the city.

🏃 Activities

Skydive Ballistic Blondes   ADVENTURE SPORTS
(☑ 0800 695 867; www.skydiveballisticblondes.co.nz; per skydive $199-380) Not only is this the oddest-named skydiving outfit in the country, it's also the only one licensed to land on the beach (Ocean Beach Ruakaka or Paihia).

Pacific Coast Kayaks   KAYAKING
(☑ 09-436 1947; www.nzseakayaking.co.nz; hire 4/8hr $60/80, tours $40-140) Hires kayaks and offers guided paddles to various Whangarei region locations.

☞ Tours

Pupurangi Hire & Tour   CULTURAL TOUR
(☑ 0800 538 891, 09-438 8117; www.hirentour.co.nz; Jetty 1, Riverside Dr; ⊙ 9.30am-5.30pm daily Oct-Apr, Sat & Sun May-Sep) Various hour-long tours of Whangarei, all with a Māori flavour, including *waka* (canoe) trips on the river ($35). Also hires kayaks (per hour $17), *waka* ($25), aquacycles ($17) and bikes ($15).

Terenga Paraoa   CULTURAL TOUR
(☑ 09-430 3083; departs Town Basin; adult/child morning $55/30, afternoon $32/20; ⊙ 9.30am & 1pm) Guided Māori cultural tours taking in Whangarei Harbour, Mt Manaia, the Kauri Park and, in the mornings, Parihaka *pa* (fortified villages).

🛏 Sleeping

Whangarei Falls Holiday Park & Backpackers   HOSTEL $
(☑ 09-437 0609; www.whangareifalls.co.nz; 12 Ngunguru Rd, Glenbervie; sites $19, dm $28-32, cabins $62-72; ⊛ ⊠) Located 5km from central Whangarei, but a short walk from Whangarei Falls, with good-value cabins and dorms, some with small kitchenettes. There's also room for tents and campervans. It's also part of the YHA network.

Whangarei Top 10   HOLIDAY PARK $
(☑ 09-437 6856; www.whangareitop10.co.nz; 24 Mair St; sites from $22, units $68-160; @ ⊛) This centrally located riverside holiday park has friendly owners, a better-than-average set of units, and super-shiny stainless-steel surfaces. Mair St is off Hatea Dr, north of the city centre.

Whangarei Views   APARTMENT $$
(☑ 09-437 6238; www.whangareiviews.co.nz; 5 Kensington Heights Rise; apt $159; ⊛) Modern and peaceful, with a self-contained two-bedroom apartment and a friendly welcome from the well-travelled Swiss-British owners. To get here, take Rust Ave, turn right into Western Hills Dr and then left into Russell Rd. Kensington Heights Rise is off

Whangarei

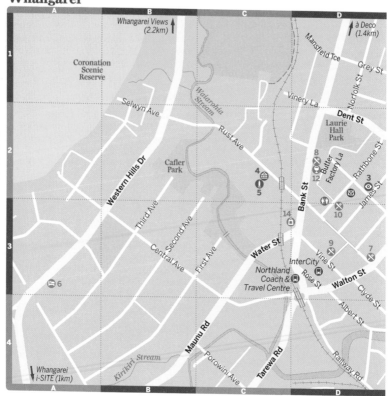

Russell Rd. There's a minimum two-night stay, and yes, the views are excellent.

Lodge Bordeaux
MOTEL $$$

(📞09-438 0404; www.lodgebordeaux.co.nz; 361 Western Hills Dr; apt $390-460; @ 🛜) Lodge Bordeaux has tasteful units with stellar kitchens and bathrooms (most with spa baths), private balconies and access to excellent wine. To get here, take Rust Ave and turn left into Western Hills Dr.

🍴 Eating

La Familia
CAFE $

(www.lafamilia.nz; 84 Cameron St; mains $10-16, pizza $13-21; ⊙7am-4pm Tue-Sat, 9am-2.30pm Sun) Versatility rules at this cosy corner location. Good pastries, counter food and coffee segue into robust Italian-themed mains and pizzas for lunch. There's a compact wine list and a good selection of beers.

Nectar
CAFE $

(📞09-438 8084; www.nectarcafe.co.nz; 88 Bank St; mains $12-20; ⊙7am-3pm Mon-Fri, 8am-2pm Sat; 🍴) 🍴 Nectar offers the winning combination of friendly staff, fair-trade coffee, and generous servings from a menu full of Northland produce. Check out the urban views from the back windows, and settle in for a lazy brunch of eggs Benedict served on chewy bagels. Vegan and organic ingredients all feature.

Nomad
MOROCCAN $$

(📞09-955 1146; www.nomadcafe.co.nz; Quality St Mall, 71 Cameron St; mains $24-28; ⊙5pm-late Tue-Sat) In a pedestrian laneway lined with cafes and restaurants, the menu standouts at this chic Moroccan-themed bar and eatery include spicy prawns, kofta and tagines. 'Dining & Vibe' is the claim on the window, and we can only agree.

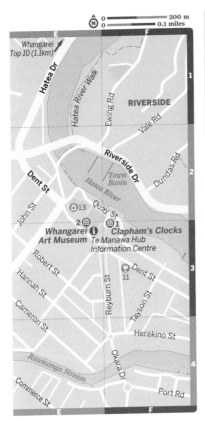

Whangarei

Top Sights
1 Clapham's Clocks F3
2 Whangarei Art Museum E3

Sights
3 Hundertwasser HQ D2
4 Old Library Arts Centre C2
5 Pou C2

Sleeping
6 Lodge Bordeaux A3

Eating
7 La Familia D3
8 Nectar D2
9 Nomad D3
10 Pimarn Thai D3

Drinking & Nightlife
11 Brauhaus Frings F3
12 Old Stone Butter Factory D2

Shopping
13 Bach E2
14 Tuatara C3

Pimarn Thai THAI $$
(☎09-430 0718; www.pimarnthai.co.nz; 12 Rathbone St; mains $16-23; ⏲11am-2.30pm Mon-Sat, from 5pm daily; ☑) As gaudy as every good Thai restaurant should be, Pimarn features all of Thailand's blockbuster dishes, including an excellent *yum talay* (spicy seafood salad).

★ **à Deco** MODERN NZ $$$
(☎09-459 4957; www.facebook.com/adeco.restaurant; 70 Kamo Rd; mains $37-42; ⏲noon-3pm Fri, 6pm-late Tue-Sat) Northland's best restaurant offers an inventive menu that prominently features local produce, including plenty of seafood. Art-deco fans will adore the setting – a wonderfully curvaceous marine-style villa with original fixtures. To get here, head north on Bank St and veer left into Kamo Rd. Bookings recommended.

Drinking & Nightlife

Old Stone Butter Factory BAR
(☎09-430 0044; www.thebutterfactory.co.nz; 84 Bank St; ⏲10am-late) Occupying a converted bank building, this cool basement bar hosts live gigs from Thursday to Saturday. As the hours dissolve, DJs kick in. It's also popular for touring Kiwi bands and musos, and has local craft beers and wine. Burgers and pizza are good value, and the sunny courtyard is ideal for a coffee. Check Facebook for what's on.

Brauhaus Frings PUB
(☎09-438 4664; www.frings.co.nz; 104 Dent St; ⏲10am-10pm) This popular pub brews its own beers, and has a terrace, wood-fired pizzas, and live music on Wednesday (jam night) and from 7pm Friday to Sunday. It's usually closed by 10pm on weekdays, but can push on to 3am on weekends.

Shopping

Tuatara ARTS, CRAFTS
(☎09-430 0121; www.tuataradesignstore.co.nz; 29 Bank St; ⏲9.30am-4.30pm Mon-Fri, 8am-2pm Sat) Māori and Pasifika design, art and craft.

Bach ARTS, CRAFTS

(☑ 09-438 2787; www.thebach.gallery; Town Basin; ⊙ 9.30am-4.30pm) Co-op store representing over 100 Northland artisans.

ℹ Information

DOC Office (☑ 09-470 3300; www.doc.govt. nz; 2 South End Ave, Raumanga; ⊙ 8am-4pm Mon-Fri) For South End Ave, turn right off SH1 around 2km south of central Whangarei.

Te Manawa Hub Information Centre (☑ 09-430 1188; Town Basin; ⊙ 9am-5pm Mon-Fri, 9am-4.30pm Sat & Sun; 🛜) Central branch of the i-SITE, in the foyer of the Whangarei Art Museum.

Whangarei i-SITE (☑ 09-438 1079; www. whangareinz.com; 92 Otaika Rd (SH1); ⊙ 9am-5pm Mon-Fri, 9am-4.30pm Sat & Sun; 🛜) Information, cafe, toilets and internet access.

Tutukaka Coast & the Poor Knights Islands

At the Poor Knights Islands, stunning underwater scenery combines with two decommissioned navy ships that have been sunk for divers to explore.

Following the road northeast of Whangarei for 26km, you'll first come to the sweet village of Ngunguru near the mouth of a broad river. Tutukaka, with its marina, is 1km further on.

From Tutukaka the road heads slightly inland, popping out 10km later at the golden sands of Matapouri. A blissful 20-minute coastal walk leads from here to Whale Bay, fringed with giant pohutukawa trees.

🏃 Activities

Dive! Tutukaka DIVING

(☑ 0800 288 882; www.diving.co.nz; Marina Rd; 2 dives incl gear $269) 🤿 Dive courses including a five-day PADI open-water course. For non-divers, there is the Perfect Day Ocean Cruise ($169) that includes lunch and snacks, snorkelling in the marine reserve, kayaking through caves and arches, paddleboarding, and sightings of dolphins (usually) and whales (occasionally). Cruises run from November to May, departing at 11am and returning at 4pm.

Tutukaka Surf Experience SURFING

(☑ 021 227 0072; www.tutukakasurf.co.nz; Marina Rd; 2hr lesson $75) Runs surf lessons at 9.30am most days in summer and on the weekends otherwise, operating from whichever beach has the best beginner breaks that day. Sandy Bay is usually popular. Also hires surfboards (per day $45) and stand-up paddle boards (per day $20). Trips leave from Tutukaka in a cool retro-style surf van.

🛌 Sleeping & Eating

Lupton Lodge B&B $$

(☑ 09-437 2989; www.luptonlodge.co.nz; 555 Ngunguru Rd; s $125-155, d $150-260, apt $275-385; 🛜🏊) The rooms are spacious, luxurious and full of character in this historic homestead (1896), peacefully positioned in farmland halfway between Whangarei and Ngunguru. Wander the orchard, splash around the pool or shoot some snooker in the guest lounge. Also available is a stylish apartment – for up to four people – in a renovated barn.

Marina Pizzeria PIZZA $$

(☑ 09-434 3166; www.marinapizzeria.co.nz; Tutukaka Marina; pizzas $18-21, mains $25-30; ⊙ 4pm-late Fri, 10am-late Sat & Sun) Everything is homemade at this excellent takeaway and restaurant – the bread, the pizza and the ice cream. Hearty breakfasts are served from 10am on weekends. Look forward to a concise but well-chosen selection of craft beer and cider. Longer hours during summer and on public holidays.

Schnappa Rock CAFE $$

(☑ 09-434 3774; www.schnapparock.co.nz; cnr Marina Rd & Marlin Pl; breakfast & lunch $13-29, dinner $27-35, bar snacks $8-19; ⊙ 8am-late, closed Sun night Jun-Sep) 🤿 Filled with expectant divers in the morning and those who are capping off their Perfect Days in the evening, this cafe-restaurant-bar is often buzzing. Top NZ bands sometimes perform on summer weekends.

BAY OF ISLANDS

The Bay of Islands ranks as one of New Zealand's top tourist drawcards, and the turquoise waters of the bay are punctuated by around 150 undeveloped islands. In particular, Paihia has excellent budget accommodation, and boat trips and water sports are very popular.

The Bay of Islands is also a place of enormous historical significance. Māori knew it as Pewhairangi and settled here early in their migrations. As the site of New Zealand's first permanent British settlement (lo-

Bay of Islands

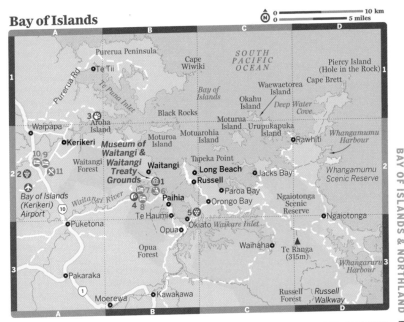

Bay of Islands

cated at Russell), it is the birthplace of European colonisation in the country. It was here that the Treaty of Waitangi was drawn up and first signed in 1840; the treaty remains the linchpin of race relations in NZ today.

Russell

◎ Sights

Pompallier Mission   HISTORIC BUILDING
(☎ 09-403 9015; www.pompallier.co.nz; The Strand; tours adult/child $10/free; ☉ 10am-4pm) Built in 1842 to house the Catholic mission's printing press, this rammed-earth building in the mission's last remaining building in the

western Pacific. A staggering 40,000 books were printed here in Māori. In the 1870s it was converted into a private home, but it is now restored to its original state, complete with tannery and printing workshop.

Christ Church   CHURCH
(Church St) English naturalist Charles Darwin made a donation towards the cost of building the country's oldest church (1836). The graveyard's biggest memorial commemorates Tamati Waka Nene, a powerful Ngāpuhi chief from the Hokianga who sided against Hone Heke in the Northland War. The church's exterior has musket and cannonball holes dating from the 1845 battle.

89

Russell

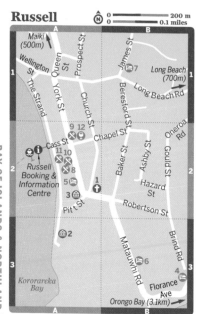

Russell

Sights
1 Christ Church A2
2 Pompallier Mission A3
3 Russell Museum A2

Sleeping
4 Arcadia Lodge B3
5 Hananui Lodge & Apartments A2
6 Russell Motel B3
7 Russell Top 10 .... B1

Eating
8 Gables A2
9 Hell Hole A2
10 Hone's Garden A2
11 Waterfront A2

Drinking & Nightlife
12 Duke of Marlborough Tavern A2

Russell Museum   MUSEUM

(☑ 09-403 7701; www.russellmuseum.org.nz; 2 York St; adult/child $10/3; ⊙ 10am-4pm) This small, modern museum has a well-presented Māori section, a large 1:5-scale model of Captain Cook's *Endeavour*, and a 10-minute video on the town's history.

Omata Estate   WINERY

(☑ 09-403 8007; www.omata.co.nz; Aucks Rd; ⊙ tastings & food 10am-5pm Nov-Mar, tastings only 11am-5pm Wed-Sun Apr-Oct) With a growing reputation for red wines – especially its old-growth syrah – Omata Estate is one of Northland's finest wineries. To complement the tastings and stunning sea views, shared platters ($40) are available. Phone ahead from April to October to confirm it's open. The winery is on the road from Russell to the car ferry at Okiato.

Tours

Russell Nature Walks   ECOTOUR

(☑ 027 908 2334; www.russellnaturewalks.co.nz; 6080 Russell Whakapara Rd; day walk adult/child $38/20, night walk $45/20; ⊙ day walk 10am, night walk varies depending on sunset) Located in privately owned native forest 2.5km south of Russell; guided day and night tours provide the opportunity to see native birds, including the weka and tui, and insects such as the weta. Glowworms softly illuminate night tours, and after dark there's the opportunity to hear (and very occasionally see) NZ's national bird, the kiwi. Walks last 1½ to two hours.

Sleeping

Russell-Orongo Bay Holiday Park   HOLIDAY PARK $

(☑ 09-403 7704; www.russellaccommodation. co.nz; 5960 Russell Rd; unpowered/powered sites $42/46, tepee $80-90, cabins & units $90-165; @ 🛜 ☻) ✐ Surrounded by 5.5 hectares studded with native forest and bird life, this relaxed holiday park is around 3km from Russell after departing the ferry from Opua to Okiato. The wide range of accommodation includes a quirky tepee and comfortable self-contained units.

Russell Top 10   HOLIDAY PARK $

(☑ 09-403 7826; www.russelltop10.co.nz; 1 James St; sites/cabins/units from $45/80/160; @ 🛜) ✐ This leafy park has a small store, good facilities, wonderful hydrangeas, tidy cabins and nice units. Showers are clean, but metered.

Russell Motel   MOTEL $$

(☑ 09-403 7854; www.motelrussell.co.nz; 16 Matauwhi Rd; units $135-210; 🛜 ☻) Sitting amid well-tended gardens, this old-fashioned motel offers a good range of units and a kidney-shaped pool that the kids will love.

The studios are a little dark, but you really can't quibble for this price in central Russell.

Arcadia Lodge
B&B $$$

(☑ 09-403 7756; www.arcadialodge.co.nz; 10 Florance Ave; d $215-300; 🐾) 🍃 The characterful rooms of this 1890 hillside house are decked out with interesting antiques and fine linen, while the breakfast is probably the best you'll eat in town – organic, delicious and complemented by spectacular views from the deck.

Hananui Lodge & Apartments
MOTEL $$$

(☑ 09-403 7875; www.hananui.co.nz; 4 York St; units $150-270; 🐾) Choose between sparkling motel-style units in the trim waterside lodge or apartments in the newer block across the road. Pick of the bunch are the upstairs waterfront units with views straight over the beach.

✗ Eating

Hell Hole
CAFE $

(☑ 022 604 1374; www.facebook.com/hellholecoffee; 16 York St; snacks $6-12; ☺ 7am-5pm mid-Dec–Feb, 8am-3pm Mar, Apr & Oct–mid-Dec) Bagels, baguettes and croissants all feature with the best coffee in town at this compact spot one block back from the waterfront. Beans are locally roasted and organic soft drinks and artisan ice blocks all combine to make Hell Hole a hugely popular place, especially during Russell's peak season from mid-December to February.

★ Gables
MODERN NZ $$

(☑ 09-403 7670; www.thegablesrestaurant.co.nz; 19 The Strand; lunch $23-29, dinner $27-34; ☺ noon-3pm Fri-Mon, from 6pm Thu-Mon) Serving an imaginative take on Kiwi classics (lamb, venison, seafood), the Gables occupies an 1847 building on the waterfront, built using whale vertebrae for foundations. Ask for a table by the windows for maritime views and look forward to local produce, including oysters and cheese. Cocktails are summery and there's a decent selection of NZ beer and wine.

Waterfront
CAFE $$

(www.waterfrontcafe.co.nz; 23 The Strand; mains $11-20; ☺ 8am-4pm; 🐾) Your best bet for a big breakfast and the first coffee of the day is this spot with brilliant harbour views. Secure a seat at one of the absolute waterfront tables and keep an eye out for dolphins showing off around the nearby wharf.

Hone's Garden
PIZZA $$

(☑ 022 466 3710; www.facebook.com/hones garden; York St; pizza $18-25, wraps & salads $14-16; ☺ noon-late summer only) Head out to Hone's pebbled courtyard for wood-fired pizza (with 11 different varieties), cold craft beer on tap and a thoroughly easygoing Kiwi vibe. An expanded menu now also features tasty wraps and healthy salads. Antipasto platters ($29 to $45) are good for groups and indecisive diners.

🍺 Drinking & Nightlife

Duke of Marlborough Tavern
PUB

(☑ 09-403 7831; www.duketavern.co.nz; 19 York St; ☺ noon-late) A cool, cosy tavern with pool tables and a local's vibe. Pub quiz on a Tuesday night (from 7pm) is always good fun, and there are well-priced burgers and fish and chips.

❶ Information

Russell Booking & Information Centre (☑ 09-403 8020, 0800 633 255; www.russell info.co.nz; Russell Pier; ☺ 8am-5pm, extended hours in summer) Loads of ideas for how to explore the area.

Paihia & Waitangi

◉ Sights

★ Waitangi Treaty Grounds
HISTORIC SITE

(☑ 09-402 7437; www.waitangi.org.nz; 1 Tau Henare Dr; adult/child $40/20; ☺ 9am-5pm Mar-24 Dec, 9am-6pm 26 Dec-Feb) 🍃 On this headland in 1840, 43 Māori chiefs, after much discussion, signed the Treaty of Waitangi with the British Crown; eventually, over 500 chiefs would sign it. Admission includes a guided tour and cultural performance, and also entry to the new Museum of Waitangi. Admission for NZ residents is $20 upon presentation of a passport or driver's licence.

★ Museum of Waitangi
MUSEUM

(☑ 09-402 7437; www.waitangi.org.nz; 1 Tau Henare Dr; adult/child $40/20; ☺ 9am-5pm Mar-24 Dec, 9am-6pm 26 Dec-Feb) The new Museum of Waitangi is a modern and comprehensive showcase of the role of the Treaty of Waitangi in the past, present and future of New Zealand. The second storey is comprised of the Ko Waitangi Tēnei (This is Waitangi) exhibition and the ground floor features special temporary exhibitions and an education

Paihia

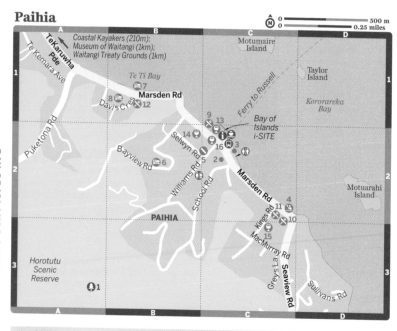

Paihia

◎ Sights
1 Opua Forest..A3

⊕ Activities, Courses & Tours
2 Explore NZ...C2
3 Fullers Great Sights...........................C2
4 Island Kayaks & Bay Beach Hire..........C2
5 Paihia Dive..C2

🛏 Sleeping
6 Allegra House......................................B2
7 Paihia Beach Resort & Spa................B1
8 Seaspray Suites...................................B1

⊗ Eating
9 35 Degrees South................................C1
10 Alfresco's...C2
11 El Cafe..C2
Paihia Farmers Market..................(see 2)
12 Provenir...B1

⦿ Drinking & Nightlife
13 Alongside..C2
14 Bay of Islands Swordfish
Club...B2
15 Pipi Patch Bar.......................................C3
16 Sauce..C2

centre. Many *taonga* (treasures) associated with Waitangi were previously scattered around NZ, and this excellent museum is now a safe haven for a number of key historical items.

Admission incorporates entry to the Waitangi Treaty Grounds (p91), a guided tour and a cultural performance.

Opua Forest   FOREST
Just behind Paihia, this regenerating forest has walking trails ranging from 10 minutes to five hours. A few large trees have escaped axe and fire, including some big kauri. Walk up from School Rd for about 30 minutes to good lookouts. Information on Opua Forest walks is available from the i-SITE. Drive into the forest by taking Oromahoe Rd west from Opua.

Haruru Falls   WATERFALL
(Haruru Falls Rd) A walking track (one way 1½ hours, 5km) leads from the Treaty Grounds along the Waitangi River to these attractive horseshoe falls. Part of the path follows a boardwalk through the mangroves. Otherwise you can drive here, turning right off Puketona Rd onto Haruru Falls Rd.

Activities

Coastal Kayakers
KAYAKING

(☑0800 334 661; www.coastalkayakers.co.nz; Te Karuwha Pde, Paihia) Runs guided tours (half-/full day $89/139, minimum two people) and multiday adventures. Kayaks (half-/full day $40/50) can also be rented for independent exploration.

Island Kayaks
& Bay Beach Hire
KAYAKING, BOATING

(☑09-402 6078; www.baybeachhire.co.nz; Marsden Rd, Paihia; half-day kayaking tour $79; ⊙9am-5.30pm) Hires kayaks (from $15 per hour), sailing catamarans ($50 first hour, $40 per additional hour), motor boats ($85 first hour, $25 per additional hour), mountain bikes ($35 per day), boogie boards ($25 per day), fishing rods ($10 per day), wetsuits and snorkelling gear (both $20 per day).

Paihia Dive
DIVING

(☑0800 107 551, 09-402 7551; www.divenz.com; Williams Rds, Paihia; dives from $239) Combined reef and wreck trips to either the *Canterbury* or the *Rainbow Warrior*.

Tours

Fullers Great Sights
CRUISE

(☑0800 653 339; www.dolphincruises.co.nz; Paihia Wharf) ⦿ The four-hour Dolphin Cruise (adult/child $105/53) departs Paihia daily at 9am and 1.30pm, offering the chance to see dolphins en route to the Hole in the Rock, and stopping at Urupukapuka Island on the way back. The four-hour Dolphin Eco Experience (adult/child $117/58, departs 8am and 12.30pm) is focused on finding dolphins to swim with.

Explore NZ
CRUISE, SAILING

(☑09-402 8234; www.explorenz.co.nz; cnr Marsden & Williams Rds, Paihia) ⦿ The four-hour Swim with the Dolphins Cruise (adult/child $95/50, additional $15 to swim) departs Paihia at 8am and 12.30pm from November to April. The four-hour Discover the Bay Cruise (adult/child $115/65) departs at 9am and 1.30pm, heading to the Hole in the Rock and stopping at Urupukapuka Island. There are also combo options available including a bus trip along Ninety Mile Beach. Explore NZ is licensed by NZ's Department of Conservation to run dolphin tours.

Sleeping

Bay of Islands Holiday Park
HOLIDAY PARK $

(☑09-402 7646; www.bayofislandsholidaypark.co.nz; 678 Puketona Rd; sites/units from $38/74; @🛜🏊) Under tall trees by a set of shallow rapids on the Waitangi River, 7km down Puketona Rd, this holiday park has excellent cabins and shady campsites.

Seaspray Suites
BOUTIQUE HOTEL $$

(☑09-402 0013; www.seaspray.co.nz; 138 Marsden Rd; d from $210; 🛜) One of the best of the phalanx of motels and apartments lining the Paihia waterfront, Seaspray Suites has chic and modern self-contained one- and two-bedroom options, some with sea-view balconies or private courtyards.

Baystay B&B
B&B $$

(☑09-402 7511; www.baystay.co.nz; 93a Yorke Rd, Haruru Falls; r $140-175; @🛜) Enjoy valley views from the spa pool of this slick, gay-friendly establishment. Yorke Rd is off Puketona Rd, just before the falls. Minimum stay of two nights; no children under 12 years.

Cook's Lookout
MOTEL $$

(☑09-402 7409; www.cookslookout.co.nz; Causeway Rd; r $175, apt $295; 🛜🏊) Cook's Lookout is an old-fashioned motel with friendly owners, breathtaking views and a solar-heated swimming pool. Take Puketona Rd towards Haruru Falls, turn right into Yorke Rd and then take the second right.

Paihia Beach Resort & Spa
APARTMENT $$$

(☑0800 870 111; 130 Marsden Rd; d $555-664; 🛜🏊) Stylish and modern studio apartments feature at this recently renovated accommodation with all suites enjoying sea views. An elegant downstairs piazza includes a swimming pool, and luxury spa services are also available. The resort's Provenir restaurant is one of Paihia's best spots for fine dining. Check online for good-value packages and last-minute discounts.

Allegra House
B&B $$$

(☑09-402 7932; www.allegra.co.nz; 39 Bayview Rd; r $245-270, apt $285; 🛜) Offering quite astonishing views of the bay from an eyrie high above the township, Allegra has three handsome B&B rooms and a spacious self-contained apartment.

Eating

El Cafe
SOUTH AMERICAN $

(☑ 09-402 7637; www.facebook.com/elcafepaihia; 2 Kings Rd; snacks & mains $5-15; ☺ 8am-4pm Tue-Thu, to 9.30pm Fri-Sun; ☎) Excellent Chilean-owned cafe with the best coffee in town and terrific breakfast burritos, tacos and baked egg dishes, such as spicy huevos rancheros. Say *hola* to owner Javier for us. His Cuban pulled-pork sandwich is truly a wonderful thing. The fruit smoothies are also great on a warm Bay of Islands day.

Paihia Farmers Market
MARKET $

(www.bayofislandsfarmersmarket.org.nz; Village Green; ☺ 2-5.30pm Thu) Stock up on local fruit, vegetables, pickles, preserves, honey, fish, smallgoods, eggs, cheese, bread, wine and oil, straight from the producers.

35 Degrees South
SEAFOOD $$

(☑ 09-402 6220; www.35south.co.nz; 69 Marsden Rd; shared plates $15-18, mains $28-26; ☺ 11.30am-late) Service can be a bit disorganised, but you can't beat the over-the-water location in central Paihia. The menu is at its best with local oysters from nearby Orongo Bay, local seafood and the shared small plates. Try the salt-and-pepper squid and pan-fried scallops, and maybe share a dessert of Dutch raisin doughnuts.

Alfresco's
PUB FOOD $$

(☑ 09-402 6797; www.alfrescosrestaurantpaihia.com; 6 Marsden Rd; breakfast & lunch $12-20, dinner $18-33; ☺ 8am-late) Locals flock to this casual restaurant-cafe-bar for great food – including lots of local seafood – and reasonable prices. Settle in for live music from 3pm to 6pm every Sunday afternoon. There's happy-hour bar prices from 3pm to 6pm every day, too.

Provenir
MODERN NZ $$$

(☑ 09-402 0111; www.paihiabeach.co.nz; 130 Marsden Rd, Paihia Beach Resort & Spa; mains $32-34; ☺ 8-10.30am & 6pm-late) A concise seasonal menu of main dishes showcases local seafood and regional NZ produce, and subtle Asian influences underpin smaller plates, including scallops and plump oysters from nearby Orongo Bay. The wine list is one of Northland's best, and during summer dining poolside is where you want to be.

Provenir is also open for 'Revive at Five' from 5pm to 7pm for a combination of classy bar snacks, beer and wine, all at a well-priced $8 each.

🍷 Drinking & Nightlife

God bless backpackers: they certainly keep the bars buzzing. There are plenty of places along Kings Rd and in the town centre to explore, so don't feel hemmed in by our list.

Alongside
BAR

(☑ 09-402 6220; www.alongside35.co.nz; 69 Marsden Rd; ☺ 8am-10pm) Quite possibly the biggest deck in all of Northland extends over the water, and a versatile approach to entertaining begins with coffee and bagels for breakfast before the inevitable transformation of Alongside into a very enjoyable bar. There's good bar snacks and meals on offer, and lots of comfy lounges are ready for conversations fuelled by cocktails or cold beer.

Sauce
CRAFT BEER

(☑ 09-402 7590; www.facebook.com/saucepizzaandcraft; Marsden Rd; ☺ 11am-10pm) Design-your-own pizzas (pizza $12 to $22) plus the added attraction of excellent craft beer on tap from Hamilton's Good George Brewery, and a few well-chosen bottles from other smaller Kiwi breweries.

Pipi Patch Bar
BAR

(☑ 09-402 7111; www.facebook.com/basebayofislands; 18 Kings Rd; ☺ 5pm-late) The party hostel has the party bar: a popular spot with large video screens and a decent terrace. You'll be shuffled inside at midnight to keep the neighbours happy – although most of them are backpackers who'll be here anyway.

Bay of Islands Swordfish Club
BAR

(Swordy; ☑ 09-403 7857; www.swordfish.co.nz; upstairs, 96 Marsden Rd; ☺ 4.30pm-late) Great views, cold beer and tall tales abound at this brightly lit club-bar where creatures from the deep protrude from every available surface. Decent burgers, steaks and seafood ($15 to $28) are also served.

ⓘ Information

Bay of Islands i-SITE (☑ 09-402 7345; www.northlandnz.com; Marsden Rd; ☺ 8am-5pm Mar–mid-Dec, 8am-7pm mid-Dec–Feb) Information and bookings.

Kerikeri

Kerikeri

 Sights

★**Stone Store**   HISTORIC BUILDING
(☑ 09-407 9236; www.historic.org.nz; 246 Kerikeri
Rd; ◷ 10am-4pm) The Stone Store (1836) sells
interesting Kiwiana gifts as well as the type
of goods that used to be sold in the store.
Tours of the wooden **Mission House** (www.
historic.org.nz; tours $10), NZ's oldest building
(1822), depart from here and include entry
to the Soul Trade exhibition on the 1st floor
of the store.

Aroha Island   WILDLIFE RESERVE
(☑ 09-407 5243; www.arohaisland.co.nz; 177 Ran-
gitane Rd; ◷ 9.30am-5.30pm) 🌿**FREE** Reached
via a permanent causeway through the
mangroves, this 5-hectare island provides
a haven for the North Island brown kiwi
and other native birds, as well as a pleasant
picnic spot for their nonfeathered admirers.
It has a visitor centre, kayaks for rent, and
after-dark walks to spy kiwi in the wild (per
person $35) can also be arranged. You have
around a 50% chance of seeing a kiwi, and
booking ahead is essential.

Ake Ake   WINERY
(☑ 09-407 8230; www.akeakevineyard.co.nz; 165
Waimate North Rd; tastings $5; ◷ cellar door 10am-

4.30pm, restaurant noon-3pm & 6-9pm Mon-Sat,
noon-3pm Sun, reduced hours outside summer)
Has free wine tastings with lunch or purchase of wine, and an excellent restaurant
(mains $28 to $34, lunch platters $25 to
$48). Phone ahead for opening hours out-
side of the summer months. Free overnight
parking is available in the vineyard grounds
for self-contained vehicles, and there's also a
1km self-guided walking trail exploring the
vineyard.

Rewa's Village   MUSEUM
(☑ 09-407 6454; www.rewasvillage.co.nz; Landing
Rd; adult/child $10/5; ◷ 10am-4pm) Take the
footbridge across the river to this mock-up
of a traditional Māori fishing village.

🏃 **Activities**

Kerikeri River Track   WALKING
Starting from Kerikeri Basin, this 4km-long
track leads past **Wharepuke Falls** and the
Fairy Pools to the **Rainbow Falls**, where the
sheet of water encloses a moss-covered cav-
ern. Alternatively, you can reach the Rainbow Falls from Rainbow Falls Rd, in which
case it's only a 10-minute walk.

Dive North   DIVING
(☑ 09-402 5369; www.divenorth.co.nz; 1512
Springbank Rd; reef & wreck $235) Based in Ker-
ikeri but offering free pick-ups from Paihia.

Kerikeri

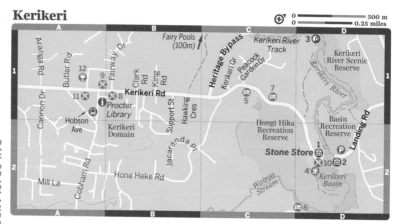

Kerikeri

◉ Top Sights
1 Stone Store......................................D2

◎ Sights
Mission House...........................(see 1)
2 Rewa's Village.................................D2
3 Wharepuke Falls D1

◐ Activities, Courses & Tours
4 Kerikeri River Track.......................D2

⊜ Sleeping
5 Bed of Roses..................................C1
6 Pagoda Lodge................................D2
7 Wharepuke Subtropical
   Accommodation C1

⊗ Eating
8 Cafe Jerusalem B1
9 Fishbone..A1
   Food at Wharepuke ....(see 7)
10 Pear Tree.....................................D2
   Village Cafe...............................(see 8)
11 Ziezo...A1

◉ Drinking & Nightlife
12 La Taza Del Diablo A1

☞ Tours

Total Tours   FOOD
(☎0800 264 868; www.totaltours.co.nz) Explore
around Kerikeri by going on a half-day food,
wine and craft tour ($70) or half-day wine
tour ($80).

⊨ Sleeping

Aroha Island   CAMPGROUND $
(☎09-407 5243; www.arohaisland.co.nz; 177 Rangi-
tane Rd; sites/units from $20/160) ✐ Kip among
the kiwi on the eco island of love *(aroha)*.
There's a wide range of reasonably priced
options, from the peaceful campsites with
basic facilities by the shelly beach, to a whole
house. The entire island, indoors and out, is
nonsmoking.

Relax a Lodge   HOMESTAY $
(☎09-407 6989; www.relaxalodge.co.nz; 1574
Springbank Rd (SH10); s $55, d & tw $70, cottages
$110-145; @🛜⛲) Less a farm, and more an
orange grove, this quiet rural house 4km out
of town sleeps just 12 people and is a cosy
and welcoming place. Some recently refur-
bished cottages dotted around the property
are also very good value.

Kauri Park   MOTEL $$
(☎09-407 7629; www.kauripark.co.nz; 512 Ker-
ikeri Rd; units $140-170; 🛜⛲) Hidden behind
tall trees on the approach to Kerikeri, this
well-priced motel has a mixture of units of
varying layouts. The premium suites are
extremely comfortable, but all options are
good value and stylishly furnished.

**Wharepuke Subtropical
Accommodation**   CABIN $$
(☎09-407 8933; www.accommodation-bay-of-
islands.co.nz; 190 Kerikeri Rd; cabins $150; 🛜) ✐
Best known for its food and lush gardens,
Wharepuke also rents five self-contained
one-bedroom cottages hidden among the
palms. They have the prefabricated look of

holiday-park cabins, but are a step up in terms of fixtures and space.

Pagoda Lodge
LODGE, CAMPGROUND **$$**

(☑ 09-407 8617; www.pagoda.co.nz; 81 Pa Rd; sites/safari tent/caravan from $40/120/130, apt $120-350; ☎) Built in the 1930s by an oddball Scotsman with an Asian fetish, this lodge features pagoda-shaped roofs grafted onto wooden cottages. The property descends to the river and is dotted with Buddhas, gypsy caravans, and safari tents with proper beds, or you can pitch your own. To get here, take Cobham Rd, turn left into Kerikeri Inlet Rd and then left into Pa Rd.

Bed of Roses
B&B **$$$**

(☑ 09-407 4666; www.bedofroses.co.nz; 165 Kerikeri Rd; r $295-475; ☎) It's all petals and no thorns at this stylish B&B, furnished with French antiques, luxe linens and comfy beds. The house has an art-deco ambience and awesome views.

Eating

Village Cafe
CAFE **$**

(☑ 09-407 4062; www.facebook.com/thevillage cafekerikeri; Village Mall, 85 Kerikeri Rd; mains $10-18; ⊘8am-4pm Mon-Fri, 8am-2pm Sat & Sun) This chic and cosmopolitan spot is popular with locals for good coffee, freshly prepared counter food, and a relaxed menu of brunch and lunch dishes. Grab a table outside in the Northland sunshine, and order the hearty potato hash.

Old Packhouse Market
MARKET **$**

(☑ 09-401 9588; www.theoldpackhousemarket. co.nz; 505 Kerikeri Rd; ⊘8am-1.30pm Sat) Local artisans, produce growers and farmers crowd this market in an old fruit-packing shed on the outskirts of town. On a Saturday morning it's the best place in town to have a leisurely breakfast.

Cafe Jerusalem
MIDDLE EASTERN **$**

(☑ 09-407 1001; www.facebook.com/cafejerusalem; Village Mall, 85 Kerikeri Rd; snacks & mains $9-18; ⊘11am-late Mon-Sat) Northland's best falafels and lamb kebabs, all served with a smile and a social vibe. Good salads, and wine and beer are also available. Try the *shakshuka* (baked eggs in a spicy tomato sauce) for a hearty brunch.

Fishbone
CAFE **$**

(☑ 09-407 6065; www.fishbonecafe.co.nz; 88 Kerikeri Rd; mains $8-20; ⊘8am-4pm Mon-Wed,

to 8pm Thu & Fri, 8.30am-3pm Sat & Sun) Kerikeri's best brekkie spot serves excellent coffee and food. Dr Seuss fans should try the green (pesto) eggs and ham. On Thursday and Friday nights Fishbone morphs into a cosy wine bar for a few hours from 4pm.

★ Food at Wharepuke
CAFE **$$**

(☑ 09-407 8936; www.foodatwharepuke.co.nz; 190 Kerikeri Rd; breakfast $14-22, lunch & dinner $24-39; ⊘10am-10.30pm Tue-Sun) With one foot in Europe, the other in Thailand and its head in the lush vegetation of Wharepuke Subtropical Gardens, this is Kerikeri's most unusual and inspired eatery. On Friday nights it serves popular Thai banquets (three courses $47.50), while on Sunday afternoons it often hosts live jazz. Adjacent is the interesting Wharepuke Print Studio & Gallery.

Ziezo
BISTRO **$$**

(☑ 09-407 9511; 55 Kerikeri Rd; mains $19-28; ⊘3pm-late Thu-Sat, from 10am Sun) This stylish bistro with glam and colourful decor certainly brightens up Kerikeri's retail-focused main street, and the food is equally interesting. An international menu offers Dutch pancakes or eggs Benedict for Sunday brunch, before moving on to Greek-style fish or an Indonesian beef rendang curry for dinner.

Pear Tree
INTERNATIONAL **$$**

(☑ 09-407 8479; www.thepeartree.co.nz; 215 Kerikeri Rd; mains $18-31; ⊘10am-10pm Thu-Mon) Kerikeri's best located and most upmarket restaurant occupies an old homestead right on the basin (book ahead for a table on the veranda). Mains run the gamut of tasty, meaty grills and lighter bistro favourites. Partner the venison with one of the Pear Tree's excellent range of NZ craft beers.

Drinking & Nightlife

La Taza Del Diablo
BAR

(☑ 09-407 3912; www.facebook.com/eltazadeldiablo; 3 Homestead Rd; ⊘4-9pm Sun, Tue & Wed, 11am-midnight Thu-Sat) This Mexican-style bar is about as energetic and raffish as buttoned-down Kerikeri gets with a decent selection of tequila and mezcal, Mexican beers, and just maybe Northland's best margaritas. Tacos, enchiladas and chimichangas all feature on the bar snacks menu ($10 to $18), and occasional live gigs

Mangonui
CHAMELEONSEYE / SHUTTERSTOCK ©

Māori terracing and a spectacular view of Doubtless Bay – particularly at sunrise and sunset. A walkway runs from Mill Bay to the *pa*, but you can also drive nearly to the top.

Butler Point Whaling Museum   MUSEUM
(☑0800 687 386; www.butlerpoint.co.nz; Marchant Rd, Hihi; adult/child $20/5; ☺by appointment)
A small private museum and Victorian homestead (1843) set in lovely gardens at Hihi, northeast of Mangonui. Its first owner, Captain Butler, left Dorset when he was 14 and at 24 was captain of a whaling ship. He settled here in 1839, had 13 children and became a trader, farmer, magistrate and Member of Parliament.

🛏 Sleeping

Puketiti Lodge   HOSTEL $
(☑09-406 0369; www.puketitilodge.co.nz; 10 Puketiti Dr; dm/s/d/tr $40/130/150/170; @🛜)
If this is what they mean by flashpacking, bring it on. For $40 you get a comfy bunk in a spacious six-person dorm that opens onto a large deck with awesome views, a locker big enough for the burliest backpack and, perhaps most surprisingly, breakfast. Turn inland at Midgley Rd, 6km south of Mangonui village, just after the Hihi turn-off.

Reia Taipa Beach Resort   RESORT $$
(☑0800 142 82472; www.taipabay.co.nz; 22 Taipa Point Rd, Taipa; d from $220; 🛜🏊) Recently renovated accommodation and a warm welcome combine at this spot with the option of beachfront and poolside studio units and apartments. There's also a good on-site restaurant, a tennis court and a spa pool.

Mangonui Waterfront Apartments Motel   APARTMENT $$
(☑09-406 0347; www.mangonuiwaterfront.co.nz; 88 Waterfront Dr; apt $125-225; @🛜) Sleeping two to eight people, these historic apartments on the Mangonui waterfront have loads of character, each one different but all with balconies, a sense of space and their own barbecue. Try to book 100-year-old Tahi.

Old Oak   BOUTIQUE HOTEL $$$
(☑09-406 1250; www.theoldoak.co.nz; 66 Waterfront Dr, Mangonui; d $175-275, ste $275-325; 🛜) This atmospheric 1861 kauri inn is now an elegant boutique hotel with contemporary design and top-notch furnishings. It oozes character, not least because the building is reputedly haunted.

sometimes raise the roof in this genteel town.

ⓘ Information

Procter Library (Cobham Rd; ☺8am-5pm Mon-Fri, 9am-2pm Sat; 🛜) Tourist information and free internet access.

Mangonui

◉ Sights & Activities

Grab the free *Heritage Trail* brochure from the visitor information centre for a 3km self-guided walk that takes in 22 historic sites. Other walks lead to attractive Mill Bay, west of Mangonui, and Rangikapiti Pa Historic Reserve, which has ancient

Eating

Mangonui Fish Shop FISH & CHIPS $
(☑ 09-406-0478; 137 Waterfront Dr; fish & chips around $13; ⊘ 10am-8pm; 🛜) Eat outdoors over the water at this famous chippie, which also sells smoked fish and seafood salads. Grab a crayfish salad and a cold beer, and you'll be sorted.

⭐ **Little Kitchen on the Bay** CAFE $$
(☑ 09-406 1644; www.facebook.com/littlekitchennz; 1/78 Waterfront Dr, Mangonui; breakfast & lunch $8-14, shared plates $13-16; ⊘ 7.30am-3pm Mon-Wed, to 9.30pm Thu & Fri, 8am-3pm Sat & Sun) Our favourite Doubtless Bay eatery is this cute spot just across from the harbour. During the day the sun-drenched interior has Mangonui's best coffee, excellent counter food and good mains – try the terrific burger. On Thursday and Friday nights the emphasis shifts to wine, craft beer, and shared plates such as pork empanadas and Swiss cheese beef sliders.

Thai Chef THAI $$
(☑ 09-406 1220; www.thethaimangonui.co.nz; 80 Waterfront Dr, Mangonui; mains $18-26; ⊘ 5-11pm Tue-Sun) Northland's best Thai restaurant serves zingy dishes with intriguing names such as The 3 Alcoholics, Spice Girls and Bangkok Showtime, and there's also a good range of Isaan (northeastern Thai) dishes to go with a frosty Singha beer. Actually, make that one of NZ's best Thai restaurants.

🛍 Shopping

Exhibit A ARTS, CRAFTS
(☑ 09-406 2333; www.facebook.com/exhibitamangonui; Old Courthouse, Waterfront Dr; ⊘ 10am-4.30pm) This co-op gallery showcases Far North artists.

Flax Bush ARTS, CRAFTS
(☑ 09-406 1510; www.flaxbush.co.nz; 50 Waterfront Dr, Mangonui; ⊘ 10am-5pm) Seashells, Pasifika and Māori crafts.

ℹ️ Information

Doubtless Bay Visitor Information Centre
(☑ 09-406 2046; www.doubtlessbay.co.nz; 118 Waterfront Dr, Mangonui; ⊘ 10am-5pm, reduced hours in winter) Excellent source of local information.

Cape Reinga & Ninety Mile Beach

👁 Sights

Cape Reinga LANDMARK
Standing at windswept Cape Reinga Lighthouse (a 1km walk from the car park) and looking out over the ocean engenders a real end-of-the-world feeling. As the waves break spectacularly and little tufts of cloud often cling to the ridges, giving sudden spooky chills even on hot days. Visible on a promontory slightly to the east is a spiritually significant 800-year-old pohutukawa tree; souls are believed to slide down its roots. Out of respect to the most sacred site in Māoridom, don't go near the tree and refrain from eating or drinking anywhere in the area.

Te Paki Recreation Reserve NATURE RESERVE
A large chunk of the land around Cape Reinga is part of the Te Paki Recreation Reserve managed by DOC. It's public land with free access; leave the gates as you found them and don't disturb the animals. There are 7 sq km of giant sand dunes on either side of the mouth of Te Paki Stream. Clamber up to toboggan down the dunes. During summer, Ahikaa Adventures (p100) are on hand to rent sandboards ($15).

Great Exhibition Bay BEACH
On the east coast, Great Exhibition Bay has dazzling snow-white silica dunes. There's no public road access, but some tours pay a *koha* (donation) to cross Māori farmland or approach the sand by kayak from Parengarenga Harbour.

🏃 Activities

Cape Reinga Coastal Walkway TRAMPING
Contrary to expectation, Cape Reinga isn't actually the northernmost point of the country; that honour belongs to Surville Cliffs further to the east. A walk along Te Werahi Beach to Cape Maria van Diemen (a five-hour loop) takes you to the westernmost point. This is one of many sections of the three- to four-day, 53km Cape Reinga Coastal Walkway (from Kapowairua to Te Paki Stream) that can be tackled individually.

Beautiful Tapotupotu Bay is a two-hour walk east of Cape Reinga, via Sandy Bay and the cliffs. From Tapotupotu Bay it's an eight-hour walk to Spirits Bay, one of NZ's most beautiful beaches. Both bays are also accessible by road.

☞ Tours

Far North

Outback Adventures ADVENTURE TOUR
(☎09-409 4586; www.farnorthtours.co.nz; price on application) Flexible, day-long, 4WD tours from Kaitaia/Ahipara, including morning tea and lunch. Options include visits to remote areas such as Great Exhibition Bay.

Harrisons Cape Runner ADVENTURE TOUR
(☎0800 227 373; www.harrisonscapereingatours.co.nz; adult/child $50/25) Day trips from Kaitaia along Ninety Mile Beach that include sandboarding and a picnic lunch.

Sand Safaris ADVENTURE TOUR
(☎0800 869 090, 09-408 1778; www.sandsafaris.co.nz; adult/child $50/30) Coach trips from Ahipara and Kaitaia, including sandboarding and a picnic lunch.

Ahikaa Adventures CULTURAL TOUR
(☎09-409 8228; www.ahikaa-adventures.co.nz; tours $50-190) Māori culture permeates these tours, which can include sandboarding, kayaking, fishing and pigging out on traditional *kai* (food).

🛏 Sleeping

DOC Campsites CAMPGROUND $
(www.doc.govt.nz; sites per adult/child $10/5) There are spectacularly positioned sites at Kapowairua, Tapotupotu Bay and Rarawa Beach. Only water, composting toilets and cold showers are provided. Bring a cooker, as fires are not allowed, and plenty of repellent to ward off mosquitoes and sandflies. 'Freedom/Leave No Trace' camping is allowed along the Cape Reinga Coastal Walkway.

North Wind Lodge Backpackers HOSTEL $
(☎09-409 8515; www.northwind.co.nz; 88 Otaipango Rd, Henderson Bay; dm/s/tw/d $30/60/66/80) Six kilometres down an unsealed road on the Aupouri Peninsula's east side, this unusual turreted house offers a homey environment and plenty of quiet spots on the lawn to sit with a beer and a book.

Pukenui Lodge Motel MOTEL $$
(☎09-409 8837; www.pukenuilodge.co.nz; 3 Pukenui Wharf Rd; motel d $99-125, hostel dm/d $27/70; 🖥🏊) Decent motel accommodation and the bonus of backpacker-friendly dorms and rooms in nearby Thomas House, a 1925 heritage building that was home to the first Pukenui Post Office.

Ahipara

◉ Sights

Shipwreck Bay BEACH
(Wreck Bay Rd) The best surfing is at this small cove at Ahipara's western edge, so named for shipwrecks still visible at low tide.

NICRAM SABOD / SHUTTERSTOCK ©

Cape Reinga Lighthouse (p99)

Ahipara Viewpoint
VIEWPOINT

(Gumfields Rd) This spectacular lookout on the bluff behind Ahipara is reached by an extremely rough road leading off the unsealed Gumfields Rd, which starts at the western end of Foreshore Dr.

🏃 Activities

Ahipara Adventure Centre
ADVENTURE SPORTS

(🖉 09-409 2055; www.ahiparaadventure.co.nz; 15 Takahe St) Hires sand toboggans ($10 per half day), surfboards ($30 per half day), mountain bikes ($50 per day), kayaks ($25 per hour), blokarts for sand yachting ($65 per hour) and quad-bikes ($95 per hour).

NZ Surf Bros
SURFING

(🖉 09-945 7276, 021 252 7078; www.nzsurfbros. com; c/o 90 Mile Beach Ahipara Holiday Park; surf lessons $60-120) NZ Surf Bros offers surfing lessons, plus day excursions and multiday trips that take in beaches on both the west and east coasts of Northland.

Ahipara Treks
HORSE RIDING

(🖉 09-409 4122; http://taitokerauhoney.co.nz/ahipara-horse-treks; 1/2hr $65/80) Offers beach canters, including some farm and ocean riding (when the surf permits).

🛏 Sleeping & Eating

★ Endless Summer Lodge
HOSTEL $

(🖉 09-409 4181; www.endlesssummer.co.nz; 245 Foreshore Rd; dm $34, d $78-92; @ 🛜) Across from the beach, this superb kauri villa (1880) has been beautifully restored and converted into an exceptional hostel. There's no TV, which encourages bonding around the long table and wood-fired pizza oven on the vine-covered back terrace. Body boards and sandboards can be borrowed and surfboards can be hired.

90 Mile Beach
Ahipara Holiday Park
HOLIDAY PARK $

(🖉 0800 888 988; www.ahiparaholidaypark.co.nz; 168 Takahe St; sites from $40, dm/r $28/75, units $75-135; @ 🛜) There's a large range of accommodation on offer at this holiday park, including cabins, motel units and a worn but perfectly presentable YHA-affiliated backpackers lodge. The communal hall has an open fire and colourful murals.

Beachfront
APARTMENT $$

(🖉 09-409 4007; www.beachfront.net.nz; 14 Kotare St; apt $175; 🛜) Who cares if it's a bit bourgeois for Ahipara? These two upmarket, self-contained apartments have watery views and there's direct access to the beach.

Bidz Takeaways
FISH & CHIPS $

(Takahe St; meals $7-15; ⊙ 9am-8pm) Fresh fish for sale, and the best fish, chips and burgers in town. There's also a small grocery store attached.

North Drift Cafe
CAFE $$

(🖉 09-409 4093; www.facebook.com/northdrift cafe; 3 Ahipara Rd; mains $12-29; ⊙ 7am-3pm Mon-Wed, 7am-3pm & 5pm-late Thu-Sun) Ahipara's best coffee and a hip relaxed atmosphere both feature at this cafe with a spacious and sunny deck. Brunch and lunch standouts include the zucchini and corn fritters and the giant green-lipped mussels in a green curry sauce, and over summer it's a top spot for a few beers and dinner specials, such as NZ lamb crusted with Mediterranean-style dukkah.

HOKIANGA

Rawene

There's an ATM in the 4 Square grocery store, and you can get petrol here.

◉ Sights

Clendon House
HISTORIC BUILDING

(🖉 09-405 7874; www.historic.org.nz; Clendon Esplanade; adult/child $10/free; ⊙ 10am-4pm Sun May-Oct, Sat & Sun Nov-Apr) Clendon House was built in the 1860s by James Clendon, a trader, shipowner and magistrate. After his death, his 34-year-old half-Māori widow Jane was left with a brood of kids and a whopping £5000 debt. She managed to clear the debt and her descendants remained in the house until 1972, when it passed to the NZ Historic Places Trust.

🛏 Sleeping & Eating

Rawene Holiday Park
HOLIDAY PARK $

(🖉 09-405 7720; www.raweneholidaypark.co.nz; 1 Marmon St; dm $20, sites/units from $32/65; 🛜 🛜) Tent sites shelter in the bush at this nicely managed park. The cabins are simple, with one converted into a bunkroom for backpackers (linen costs extra).

Boatshed Cafe
CAFE $

(☑ 09-405 7728; 8 Clendon Esplanade; mains $10-22; ⏱ 8.30am-4pm) Eat overlooking the water at this cafe, a cute place with excellent food and a gift shop that sells local art and crafts. The cafe sometimes opens for dinner at the weekend.

Opononi & Omapere

These tranquil settlements near the south head of Hokianga Harbour run into one another. The water's much clearer here and good for swimming, and views are dominated by the mountainous sand dunes across the water at North Head. If you're approaching Omapere from the south, the view of the harbour is nothing short of spectacular.

Activities

Arai te Uru Heritage Walk   WALKING
See p26

Jim Taranaki's Bone Carving Studio   COURSE
(☑ 09-405 8061; hokiangabonecarvingstudio@gmail.com; 15 Akiha St, Omapere; class incl lunch $60) Create your own Māori-inspired bone-carving in a studio with ocean views.

☞ Tours

Footprints Waipoua   CULTURAL TOUR
See p29

Hokianga Express   ADVENTURE SPORTS
(☑ 021 405 872, 09-405 8872; per tour $27; ⏱ 10am-2pm summer) A boat departs from Opononi Jetty and takes you across the harbour to the large golden sand dunes, where you can spend an hour sandboarding down a 30m slope or skimming over the water. Boogie boards are provided and bookings are essential. Outside of the peak season, the service is not always available.

🛏 Sleeping

GlobeTrekkers Lodge   HOSTEL $
(☑ 09-405 8183; www.globetrekkerslodge.com; SH12, Omapere; dm/s/d $28/50/60; @ ☎) Unwind in casual style at this home-style hostel with harbour views and bright dorms. Private rooms have plenty of thoughtful touches, such as writing desks, mirrors, art and fluffy towels. There's a stereo, but no TV, encouraging plenty of schmoozing in the grapevine-draped barbecue area.

Copthorne Hotel & Resort
HOTEL $$

(☑ 09-405 8737; www.milleniumhotels.co.nz; 336 SH12, Omapere; r $140-200; ☎ ⛵) Despite the original Victorian villa having been hijacked by aluminium windows, this waterside complex remains an attractive spot for a summer's drink or bistro meal ($25 to $32). The more expensive rooms in the newer accommodation block have terraces and water views. Even if you're not staying here, it's definitely worth dropping in for a drink at the cosy bar.

Check online for worthwhile midweek and off-peak specials.

★ Kokohuia Lodge   B&B $$$
(☑ 021 779 927; www.kokohuialodge.co.nz; 101 Kokohuia Rd, Omapere; d $295-320; ☎) 🌿 Luxury and sustainable, ecofriendly practices combine at this B&B, nestled in regenerating native bush high above the silvery dune-fringed expanse of the Hokianga Harbour. Solar energy and organic and free-range produce all feature, but there's no trade-off for luxury in the modern and stylish accommodation.

Hokianga Haven   B&B $$$
(☑ 09-405 8285; www.hokiangahaven.co.nz; 226 SH12, Omapere; r $220-240; ☎) This modern house with original Kiwi art on the walls offers spacious accommodation on the harbour's edge and glorious views of the sand dunes. Alternative healing therapies can be arranged, and there are accommodation discounts for stays longer than one night.

🍴 Eating

Landing   CAFE $$
(☑ 09-405 8169; www.thelandingcafe.co.nz; 29 SH12; snacks & mains $6-19; ⏱ 8.30am-3pm) Stylish Kiwiana decor combines with good cafe fare at this new opening with an expansive view-friendly deck. Try one of the hearty butter-chicken pies, or combine the mussel fritters with a dollop of locally produced relish. Salad fans will enjoy options including Israeli couscous, or a roast beetroot and feta cheese combo.

Opononi Hotel   PUB FOOD $$
(☑ 09-405 8858; www.opononihotel.com; 19 SH12; mains $18-30; ⏱ 11am-late) Options at the friendly local pub include decent pizza in the main bar, or flasher bistro meals in the attached Boar and Marlin restaurant. Either way, try and score an outside table so you can

Tane Mahuta (p28)

take in the improbable views of Opononi's massive sand dunes just across the harbour.

❶ Information

Opononi i-SITE (☑ 09-405 8869; 29 SH12; ⊗ 8.30am-5pm) Excellent information office with a good range of local souvenirs.

KAURI COAST

Waipoua Forest

The highlight of Northland's west coast, control of Waipoua Forest has been returned to Te Roroa, the local *iwi* (tribe), as part of a settlement for Crown breaches of the Treaty of Waitangi. Te Roroa runs the Waipoua Forest Visitor Centre (p28), near the south end of the park.

Another option to visit the forest is on a twilight tour, departing from Omapere with Footprints Waipoua (p29).

◉ Sights

Tane Mahuta   TREE
See p28

Te Matua Ngahere   TREE
From the Kauri Walks car park, a 20-minute (each way) walk leads past the Four Sisters, a graceful stand of four tall trees fused to-

gether at the base, to Te Matua Ngahere (the Father of the Forest). At 30m, he has a significant presence. Reinforced by a substantial girth – he's the fattest living kauri (16.4m) – the tree presides over a clearing surrounded by mature trees resembling mere matchsticks in comparison.

A 30-minute (one way) path leads from near the Four Sisters to Yakas, the seventh-largest kauri.

Waipoua Forest Visitor Centre   ARTS CENTRE
See p28

🛌 Sleeping

Waipoua Forest Campground   CAMPGROUND $
(☑ 09-439 6445; www.teroroa.iwi.nz/visit-waipoua; 1 Waipoua River Rd; sites/units/house from $15/20/175) Situated next to the Waipoua River and the visitor centre, this peaceful camping ground offers hot showers, flush toilets and a kitchen. The cabins are extremely spartan, with unmade squab beds (bring your own linen or hire it). There are also whole houses for rent, sleeping 10.

★ Waipoua Lodge   B&B $$$
(☑ 09-439 0422; www.waipoualodge.co.nz; SH12; d incl breakfast $585; 🛜) This fine old villa at the southern edge of the forest has four luxurious, spacious suites, which were originally the stables, the woolshed and the calf-rearing pen. Decadent dinners ($80) are available.

Mural of Māori warrior visiting Tane Mahuta (p28)
PAUL KENNEDY / GETTY IMAGES ©

ⓘ Information

Waipoua Forest Visitor Centre (☑ 09-439 6445; www.teroroa.iwi.nz/visit-waipoua; 1 Waipoua River Rd; ⊙ 9am-6.30pm summer, 9am-4pm winter) Waipoua Forest Visitor Centre, run by Te Roroa, is a cafe and camping ground near the south end of Waipoua Forest.

Matakohe

Kauri Museum   MUSEUM
See p29

Matakohe Pioneer Church   CHURCH
Facing the museum, this tiny kauri-built (1867) church served both Methodists and Anglicans, and acted as the community's hall and school. Nearby, you can wander through a historic school house (1878) and post office/telephone exchange (1909).

🛏 Sleeping

Matakohe Holiday Park   HOLIDAY PARK $
(☑ 09-431 6431; www.matakoheholidaypark.co.nz; 66 Church Rd; sites/units from $38/65; @ 🛜 🏊) This little park has modern amenities, plenty of space and good views of Kaipara Harbour.

Matakohe House   B&B $$
(☑ 09-431 7091; www.matakohehouse.co.nz; 24 Church Rd; d $160; 🛜) This B&B occupies a pretty villa with a cafe attached. The simply furnished rooms open out onto a veranda and offer winning touches such as complimentary port and chocolates.

Coromandel Peninsula

Coromandel's east coast has some of the North Island's best white-sand beaches. When Auckland shuts up shop for Christmas and New Year, this is where it heads.

The Coromandel Peninsula juts into the Pacific east of Auckland, forming the eastern boundary of the Hauraki Gulf. Although relatively close to the metropolis, the Coromandel offers easy access to splendid isolation. Its dramatic, mountainous spine bisects it into two very distinct parts.

The east coast has some of the North Island's best white-sand beaches. When Auckland shuts up shop for Christmas and New Year, this is where it heads. The cutesy historic gold-mining towns on the western side escape the worst of the influx, their muddy wetlands and picturesque stony bays holding less appeal for the masses. This coast has long been a refuge for alternative lifestylers. Down the middle, the mountains are criss-crossed with walking tracks, allowing trampers to explore large tracts of untamed bush where kauri trees once towered and are starting to do so again.

Thames

◉ Sights

 Goldmine Experience MINE
(☑ 07-868 8514; www.goldmine-experience.co.nz; cnr Moanataiari Rd & Pollen St; adult/child $15/5; ☉ 10am-4pm daily Jan-Mar, to 1pm Sat & Sun Apr, May & Sep-Dec) Walk through a mine tunnel, watch a stamper battery crush rock, learn about the history of the Cornish miners and try your hand at panning for gold ($2 extra).

School of Mines & Mineralogical Museum MUSEUM
(☑ 07-868 6227; www.historicplaces.org.nz; 101 Cochrane St; adult/child $10/free; ☉ 11am-3pm Wed-Sun Mar-Dec, daily Jan & Feb) The NZ Historic Places Trust runs tours of these buildings, which house an extensive collection of NZ rocks, minerals and fossils. The oldest section (1868) was part of a Methodist Sunday School, situated on a Māori burial ground. The Trust has a free self-guided tour pamphlet taking in Thames' significant buildings.

Butterfly & Orchid Garden GARDENS
(☑ 07-868 8080; www.butterfly.co.nz; Victoria St; adult/child $12/6; ☉ 9.30am-4.30pm Sep-May) Around 3km north of town within the Dickson Holiday Park is this enclosed jungle full of hundreds of exotic flappers.

🏃 Activities

Canyonz CANYONING
(☑ 0800 422 696; www.canyonz.co.nz; trips $360) 🍃 All-day canyoning trips to the Sleeping God Canyon in the Kauaeranga Valley. Expect a vertical descent of over 300m, requiring abseiling, water-sliding and jumping. Trips leave from Thames at 8.30am; 7am pick-ups from Hamilton are also available. Note that Thames is only a 1½-hour

Thames

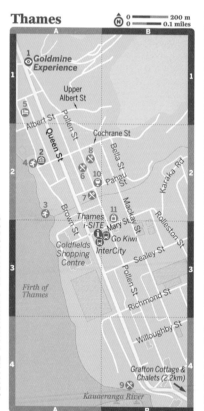

shared rooms, private singles and doubles, and a sunny garden. Breakfast is included and all rooms share bathrooms. Also on offer are shuttle services to the Pinnacles and various points along the Hauraki Rail Trail; bikes can be hired. Cars can also be rented for exploring more remote areas of the Coromandel Peninsula.

Cotswold Cottage B&B **$$**
(☏ 07-868 6306; www.cotswoldcottage.co.nz; 46 Maramarahi Rd; r $180-210; 🛜) ☕ Looking over the river and racecourse, 3km southeast of town, this pretty villa features luxuriant linen and an outdoor spa pool. The comfy rooms all open onto a deck.

Coastal Motor Lodge MOTEL **$$**
(☏ 07-868 6843; www.stayatcoastal.co.nz; 608 Tararu Rd; units $150-179; 🛜) Motel and chalet-style accommodation is provided at this smart, welcoming place, 2km north of Thames. It overlooks the sea, making it a popular choice, especially in the summer months.

Grafton Cottage & Chalets CHALET **$$**
(☏ 07-868 9971; www.graftoncottage.co.nz; 304 Grafton Rd; units $140-220; 🖥🛜🏊) Most of these attractive wooden chalets perched on a hill have decks with awesome views. The

drive from central Auckland, so with your own transport a day trip from Auckland is possible.

Thames Small Gauge Railway RAILWAY
(www.facebook.com/www.thamesrailway; Brown St; tickets $2; ⊙ 11am-3pm Sun) Young ones will enjoy the 900m loop ride on this cute-as-a-button train.

Karaka Bird Hide BIRDWATCHING
🎫 **FREE** Built with compensation funds from the *Rainbow Warrior* bombing, this hide can be reached by a boardwalk through the mangroves just off Brown St.

🛏 Sleeping

Sunkist Backpackers B&B **$**
(☏ 07-868 8808; www.sunkistbackpackers.com; 506 Brown St; dm $30-35, s/d $65/85; 🖥🛜) This character-filled 1860s heritage building has

hospitable hosts provide free internet access and breakfast, as well as use of the pool, spa and barbecue areas.

Eating

Cafe Melbourne
CAFE $

(📞07-868 3159; www.facebook.com/cafemelb ournegrahamstown; 715 Pollen St; mains $13-18; ⊙8am-5pm Mon-Thu, to 9pm Fri, 9am-4pm Sat & Sun) Stylish and spacious, this cafe definitely channels the cosmopolitan vibe of a certain Australian city. Shared tables promote a convivial ambience, and the menu travels from ricotta pancakes to beef sliders and fish curry for lunch. It's in a repurposed building called The Depot where you'll also find a juice bar and a deli with artisanal bread and takeaway salads.

Wharf Coffee House & Bar
CAFE $

(📞07-868 6828; www.facebook.com/thewharf coffeehouseandbar; Queen St, Shortland Wharf; snacks & mains $10-18; ⊙9am-3pm Mon, to 7pm Tue, Wed & Sun, to 9pm Thu-Sat) Perched beside the water, this rustic wood-lined pavilion does great fish and chips. Grab a table outside with a beer or a wine to understand why the Wharf is a firm local favourite.

Coco Espresso
CAFE $

(📞07-868 8616; 661 Pollen St; snacks from $5; ⊙7.30am-2pm Mon-Fri, 8.30am-12.30pm Sat) Occupying a corner of an old villa, this chic little cafe serves excellent coffee and enticing pastries and cakes.

Nakontong
THAI $$

(📞07-868 6821; www.nakontong.com; 728 Pollen St; mains $16-21; ⊙11am-2.30pm Mon-Fri, 5-10pm daily; 🖉) This is the most popular restaurant in Thames by a country mile. Although the bright lighting may not induce romance, the tangy Thai dishes will provide a warm glow.

Drinking & Nightlife

Junction Hotel
PUB

(📞07-868 6008; www.thejunction.net.nz; 700 Pollen St; ⊙10am-late) Serving thirsty golddiggers since 1869, the Junction is the archetypal slightly rough-around-the-edges, historic, small-town pub. Live music attracts a younger crowd on the weekends, while families head to the corner-facing Grahamstown Bar & Diner for hearty pub grub (mains $15 to $30).

Shopping

Thames Market
MARKET

(📞07-868 9841; Pollen St, Grahamstown; ⊙8am-noon Sat) 🖉 On Saturday mornings the Grahamstown market fills the street with organic produce and handicrafts.

❶ Information

Thames i-SITE (📞07-868 7284; www.thecoro mandel.com/thames; 200 Mary St; ⊙9am-5pm Mon-Fri, to 2pm Sat, 10am-4pm Sun) Excellent source of information for the entire Coromandel Peninsula.

Coromandel Town

◉ Sights

Coromandel Goldfield Centre & Stamper Battery
HISTORIC BUILDING

(📞021 0232 8262; www.coromandelstamper battery.weebly.com; 360 Buffalo Rd; adult/child $10/5; ⊙10am-4pm, tours hourly 10am-3pm, closed Fri in winter) The rock-crushing machine clatters into life during the informative tours of this 1899 plant. You can also try panning for gold ($5) and stop to see NZ's largest working waterwheel. Ask about the special summertime tours by lamplight at 5pm daily.

Coromandel Mining & Historic Museum
MUSEUM

(📞07-866 8987; 841 Rings Rd; adult/child $5/free; ⊙10am-1pm Sat & Sun Feb–mid-Dec, 10am-4pm daily mid-Dec–Jan) Small museum with glimpses of pioneer life.

ESSENTIAL COROMANDEL PENINSULA

Eat Coromandel bivalves – mussels, oysters and scallops are local specialities.

Drink Local Coromandel craft beer at Luke's Kitchen & Cafe (p109).

Read The Penguin History of New Zealand (2003) by the late Michael King, an Opoutere resident.

Watch Passing schools of fish while snorkelling near Hahei (p112).

Online www.thecoromandel.com, www.hamiltonwaikato.com, www.kingcountry.co.nz

Area code 📞07

☆ Activities

★ Driving Creek Railway & Potteries RAILWAY
See p41

Mussel Barge Snapper Safaris FISHING
(☑ 07-866 7667; www.musselbargesafaris.co.nz; adult/child $55/30) Fishing trips with a local flavour and lots of laughs. Pick-up service is available.

☞ Tours

Coromandel Adventures DRIVING TOUR
(☑ 07-866 7014; www.coromandeladventures. co.nz; 480 Driving Creek Rd; 1-day tour adult/child $80/50) Various tours around Coromandel Town and the peninsula, plus shuttles to Whitianga and Auckland.

⚏ Sleeping

Anchor Lodge MOTEL, HOSTEL $
(☑ 07-866 7992; www.anchorlodgecoromandel. co.nz; 448 Wharf Rd; dm $31, d $73, units $135-320; @ 🛜 🏊) This upmarket backpacker-motel combo has its own gold mine, glowworm cave, small heated swimming pool and spa. The 2nd-floor units have harbour views.

Coromandel Motel & Holiday Park HOLIDAY PARK $
(☑ 07-866 8830; www.coromandeltop10.co.nz; 636 Rings Rd; campsites from $46, units $80-185; @ 🛜 🏊) Well-kept and welcoming, with nicely painted cabins and manicured lawns, this large park includes the semi-separate Coromandel Town Backpackers. It gets busy in summer, so book ahead. Also hires bikes ($20 per day).

★ Hush Boutique Accommodation STUDIO $$
(☑ 07-866 7771; www.hushaccommodation.co.nz; 425 Driving Creek Rd; campervans $45, cabins & studios $145-175) Rustic but stylish studios are scattered throughout native bush at this easygoing spot. Lots of honey-coloured natural wood creates a warm ambience, and the shared Hush alfresco area with kitchen facilities and a barbecue is a top spot to catch up with fellow travellers. Hush Petite ($145) is a very cosy stand-alone one-bedroom cottage that was originally a potter's cottage.

Jacaranda Lodge B&B $$
(☑ 07-866 8002; www.jacarandalodge.co.nz; 3195 Tiki Rd; s $90, d $155-185; 🛜) 🌱 Located among 6 hectares of farmland and rose gardens, this two-storey cottage is a relaxing retreat. Look forward to excellent breakfasts from the friendly new owners, Judy and Gerard, often using produce – plums, almonds, macadamia nuts and citrus fruit – from the property's spray-free orchard. Some rooms share bathrooms.

Green House B&B $$
(☑ 07-866 7303; www.greenhousebandb.co.nz; 505 Tiki Rd; r $180; @ 🛜) Good old-fashioned hospitality with three smartly furnished rooms on offer. The pretty downstairs Garden Room has recently been refurbished, and guests enjoy sea views and a rural outlook.

✗ Eating

Driving Creek Cafe VEGETARIAN, VEGAN $
(☑ 07-866 7066; www.drivingcreekcafe.com; 180 Driving Creek Rd; mains $9-18; ⊙ 9.30am-5pm; 🛜 🌱) 🌿 Vegetarian, vegan, gluten-free, organic and fair-trade delights await at this funky mudbrick cafe. The food is beautifully presented, fresh and healthy. Once sated, the kids can play in the sandpit while the adults check their email on the free wi-fi. Don't miss ordering a terrific juice or smoothie.

Coromandel Oyster Company SEAFOOD $
(☑ 07-866 8028; 1611 Tiki Rd; snacks & meals $5-25; ⊙ 10am-5.30pm Sat-Thu, to 6.30pm Fri) Briny-fresh mussels, scallops, oysters and cooked fish and chips and flounder. Coming from Thames you'll find them on the hill around 7km before you reach Coromandel Town.

★ Coromandel Mussel Kitchen SEAFOOD $$
(☑ 07-866 7245; www.musselkitchen.co.nz; cnr SH25 & 309 Rd; mains $18-21; ⊙ 9am-3.30pm, plus dinner late Dec-Feb) This cool cafe-bar sits among fields 3km south of town. Mussels are served with Thai- and Mediterranean-tinged sauces or grilled on the half-shell. In summer the garden bar is perfect for a mussel-fritter stack and a frosty craft beer from MK Brewing Co, the on-site microbrewery. Smoked and chilli mussels and bottles of the beers are all available for takeaway.

Pepper Tree MODERN NZ $$
(☑ 07-866 8211; www.peppertreerestaurant.co.nz; 31 Kapanga Rd; mains lunch $16-28, dinner $25-39; ⊙ 10am-9pm; 🛜) Coromandel Town's most upmarket option dishes up generously pro-

Colville General Store

portioned meals with an emphasis on local seafood. On a summer's evening, the courtyard tables under the shady tree are the place to be.

 Drinking & Nightlife

Star & Garter Hotel PUB
(☑07-866 8503; www.starandgarter.co.nz; 5 Kapanga Rd; ☺11am-late) Making the most of the simple kauri interior of an 1873 building, this smart pub has pool tables, decent sounds and a roster of live music and DJs on the weekends. The beer garden is smartly clad in corrugated iron.

ℹ **Information**

Coromandel Town Information Centre (☑07-866 8598; www.coromandeltown.co.nz; 85 Kapanga Rd; ☺10am-4pm; ☎) Good maps and local information. Pick up the Historic Places Trust's *Coromandel Town* pamphlet here.

Colville

Situated 25km north of Coromandel Town, Colville is a magnet for alternative lifestylers. There's not much here except for the quaint **Colville General Store** (☑07-866 6805; Colville Rd; ☺8.30am-5pm), selling everything from organic food to petrol (warning: this is your last option for either). Another essential stop as you continue north is **Hereford 'n' a Pickle** (☑021 136 8952; www.facebook.com/hereford.n.a.pickle; pies $4-6; ☺9am-4pm; ☎). Good coffee, fresh fruit ice cream, and pies made with meat from local Hereford cattle are the standouts at this rustic self-described 'farm shop' that also boasts free wi-fi and sunny outdoor seating. Sausages and smoked meats are available to take away, along with other local produce including fresh juices, jams and pickles.

The 1260-hectare **Colville Farm** (☑07-866 6820; www.colvillefarmholidays.co.nz; 2140 Colville Rd; d $75-130; @☎) has accommodation including bare-basics bush lodges and self-contained houses. Guests can try their hands at farm work (including milking) or go on horse treks ($40 to $150, one to five hours).

Kuaotunu

In Kuaotunu village, **Luke's Kitchen & Cafe** (☑07 866 4420; www.lukeskitchen.co.nz; 20 Blackjack Rd, Kuaotunu; mains & pizza $15-28; ☺cafe & gallery 8.30am-3.30pm, restaurant & bar 11am-10pm, shorter hours in winter) has a rustic surf-shack ambience, cold brews (including craft beers from around NZ) and excellent wood-fired pizza. Occasional live music, local seafood and creamy fruit smoothies make Luke's an essential stop. Adjacent is Luke's new daytime cafe and gallery with very good coffee, home-baked goodies and eclectic local art for sale. Try the Spanish eggs or a bacon-and-egg roll in Kuaotunu sunshine and you'll be a happy traveller.

For more luxury, head back along the beach to **Kuaotunu Bay Lodge** (☑07-866 4396; www.kuaotunubay.co.nz; SH25; s/d $270/295; ⊙), an elegant B&B set among manicured gardens, offering a small set of spacious sea-gazing rooms.

Heading off the highway at Kuaotunu takes you (via an unsealed road) to one of Coromandel's best-kept secrets. First the long stretch of **Otama Beach** comes into view – deserted but for a few houses and farms. Continue along the narrowing road; the sealed road finally starts again and you reach **Opito**, a hidden-away enclave of 250 flash properties (too smart to be called baches), of which only 16 have permanent residents. From this magical beach, you can walk to the Ngāti Hei *pa* (fortified village) site at the far end.

At Opito, **Leighton Lodge** (☑07-866 0756; www.leightonlodge.co.nz; 17 Stewart Pl; s $160-190, d $200-220; ⊙) is a smart B&B with friendly owners, a self-contained flat downstairs, and an upstairs room with a view-hungry balcony.

Whitianga

◎ Sights

Buffalo Beach is on Mercury Bay, north of Whitianga Harbour. A five-minute passenger ferry ride will take you across the harbour to **Ferry Landing**. From here you can walk to local sights like **Whitianga Rock Scenic & Historical Reserve**, a park with great views over the ocean, and the **Shakespeare Cliff Lookout**. Further afield are Hahei Beach (13km), Cathedral Cove (15km) and Hot Water Beach (18km, one hour by bike). Look forward to relatively flat terrain if you're keen on riding from Ferry Landing to these other destinations.

Lost Spring   SPRING
(☑07-866 0456; www.thelostspring.co.nz; 121a Cook Dr; per 90min/day $38/68; ⊙10.30am-6pm Sun-Fri, to 8pm Sat) This expensive but intriguing Disney-meets-Polynesia thermal complex is the ideal spot to relax in tropical tranquillity, with a cocktail in hand. There's also a day spa and cafe. Children under 14 must be accompanied by an adult in the hot pools.

Mercury Bay Museum   MUSEUM
(☑07-866 0730; www.mercurybaymuseum.co.nz; 11a The Esplanade; adult/child $7.50/50¢; ⊙10am-4pm) A small but interesting museum focusing on local history – especially Whitianga's most famous visitors, Kupe and Cook.

⚡ Activities

Bike Man   BICYCLE RENTAL
(☑07-866 0745; thebikeman@xtra.co.nz; 16 Coghill St; per day $25; ⊙9am-5pm Mon-Fri, to 1pm Sat) Rent a bike to take across on the ferry and journey out to Hahei and Hot Water Beach.

Windborne   SAILING
(☑027 475 2411; www.windborne.co.nz; day sail $95; ⊙Dec-Apr) Day sails in a 19m 1928 schooner from December to April, and also departures to the Mercury Islands ($150) in February and March.

☞ Tours

There are a baffling number of tours to **Te Whanganui-A-Hei Marine Reserve**, where you'll see interesting rock formations and, if you're lucky, dolphins, fur seals, penguins and orcas. Some are straight-out cruises while others offer optional swims and snorkels. See p45 for a list of tour operators.

🛏 Sleeping

Mercury Bay Holiday Park   HOLIDAY PARK $
(☑07-866 5579; www.mercurybayholidaypark.co.nz; 121 Albert St; campsites from $23, units $85-160; ⊙❀🐾) Strangely planted in a suburban neighbourhood, this small holiday park is comfortable and clean, with playgrounds, trampoline, swimming pool and pool table.

Beachside Resort   MOTEL $$
(☑07-867 1356; www.beachsideresort.co.nz; 20 Eyre St; units $195-225; ❀🐾) Attached to the sprawling Oceans Resort, this modern motel has tidy units with kitchenettes and balconies on the upper level. Despite the name, it's set back from the beach, but it does have a heated pool.

Within the Bays   B&B $$$
(☑07-866 2848; www.withinthebays.co.nz; 49 Tarapatiki Dr; r $275-325; ❀⊙) It's the combination of charming hosts and incredible views that make this B&B set on a hill overlooking Mercury Bay really worth considering. It's extremely well set up for guests with restricted mobility – there's even a

wheelchair-accessible bush track on the property. Find it 5km from Whitianga town.

Eating

Cafe Nina
CAFE $

(📞 07-866 5440; www.facebook.com/cafenina whitianga; 20 Victoria St; mains $8-20; ⏱ 8am-3pm) Barbecue for breakfast? Why the hell not. Too cool to be constricted to four walls, the kitchen grills bacon and eggs on an outdoor hotplate while the punters spill out onto tables in the park. Other dishes include robust Greek salads and tasty quesadillas.

Blue Ginger
SOUTHEAST ASIAN $$

(📞 07-867 1777; www.blueginger.co.nz; 1/10 Blacksmith Lane; shared plates $9-14, mains $22-28; ⏱ 11am-2pm Tue-Fri & 5pm-late Tue-Sat) Southeast Asian flavours infuse the menu at this relaxed spot with shared tables. Highlights include Indonesian-style beef rendang, pad thai noodles as well as a great roast duck red curry.

Mercury Bay Estate
WINERY $$

(📞 07-866 4066; www.mercurybayestate.co.nz; 761a Purangi Rd, Cooks Beach; platters $18-48, wine tasting $8-15; ⏱ 10am-5pm Mon-Fri, 9am-6pm Sat & Sun) Repurposed timber and corrugated iron feature at this rustic but chic vineyard en route from Ferry Landing to Cooks Beach. Seafood, cheese and charcuterie platters team with wines like the excellent Lonely Bay chardonnay. Local artwork is also for sale. It's 35km from Whitianga town.

Squids
SEAFOOD $$

(📞 07-867 1710; www.squids.co.nz; 15/1 Blacksmith Lane; mains $15-32; ⏱ 11am-2.30pm & 5.30pm-late) On a corner facing the harbour, this informal restaurant offers good-value seafood meals in a prime location. Steamed mussels, smoked seafood platters and chowder combine with occasional Asian touches. The steaks are also good.

Poivre & Sel
MODERN NZ $$$

(📞 07-866 0053; www.poivresel.co.nz; 2 Mill Rd; mains $35-40; ⏱ 6pm-late Tue-Sat) This Mediterranean-style villa – complete with a garden shaded by palm trees – is the most stylish eatery in town. Begin with crab and black garlic in an avocado and grapefruit parfait before moving on to delicate porcini-stuffed quail with asparagus. Happy-hour $5 drinks from 5pm to 6pm are a good way

Whitianga

⬤ 0 ——— 200 m
0 ——— 0.1 miles

Whitianga

◉ Sights
1 Lost Spring A1
2 Mercury Bay Museum........................B2

◎ Activities, Courses & Tours
3 Bike Man A2

◎ Sleeping
4 Beachside Resort..................................A1
5 Mercury Bay Holiday Park.................A3

◎ Eating
6 Blue Ginger B2
7 Cafe Nina A2
8 Poivre & Sel A2
9 Squids...B2

◎ Drinking & Nightlife
10 Whitianga Hotel...................................B2

to kick things off. Booking for dinner is recommended.

Drinking & Nightlife

Whitianga Hotel
PUB

(📞 07-866 5818; www.whitiangahotel.co.nz; 1 Blacksmith Lane; ⏱ 11am-late) Good-value pub food, lots of frosty beers on tap and a relaxed garden bar equal a classic Kiwi pub experience.

Challenge the locals on the pool table and return on weekend nights for DJs and cover bands playing songs you'll probably know all the words to.

❶ Information

Whitianga i-SITE (☏ 07-866 5555; www.whitianga.co.nz; 66 Albert St; ⊘ 9am-5pm Mon-Fri, to 4pm Sat & Sun) Information and internet access. Hours are extended in summer.

Hahei

⊙ Sights

Cathedral Cove BEACH
Beautiful Cathedral Cove, with its famous gigantic stone arch and natural waterfall shower can be reached from Hahei Beach – it will take about 70 minutes to walk. Another option is to take the 10-minute Cathedral Cove Water Taxi (p44). Note that over the peak summer months, both the car park and the cove itself can be very busy.

Hahei Beach BEACH
Long, lovely Hahei Beach is made more magical by the view to the craggy islands in the distance. From the southern end of Hahei Beach, it's a 15-minute walk up to Te Pare, a *pa* (fortified village) site with splendid coastal views.

🏌 Activities

Cathedral Cove Sea Kayaking KAYAKING
See p45

Hahei Beach Bikes BICYCLE RENTAL
(☏ 021 701 093; www.haheibeachbikes.co.nz; 2 Margot Pl; bike hire half-/full day $35/45) Friendly owner Jonny also provides local maps with key points of interest and a spade for digging a personal spa pool at Hot Water Beach. By arrangement, bikes can be delivered to Ferry Landing to meet travellers arriving off the ferry from Whitianga.

☞ Tours

Hahei Explorer ADVENTURE TOUR
See p45

🛏 Sleeping

Tatahi Lodge HOSTEL, MOTEL $
(☏ 07-866 3992; www.tatahilodge.co.nz; Grange Rd; dm $33, r $90-130, units $140-225; @ ☏) A wonderful place where backpackers are treated

with at least as much care and respect as the lush, bromeliad-filled garden. The dorm rooms and excellent communal facilities are just as attractive as the pricier motel units.

Purangi Garden Accommodation COTTAGE $$
(☏ 07-866 4036; www.purangigarden.co.nz; Lees Rd; d $180-200) On a quiet cove on the Purangi River, this relaxing spot has accommodation ranging from comfortable chalets through to larger houses and a spacious, self-contained yurt. Well-established gardens and rolling lawns lead to the water – perfect for swimming and kayaking – and don't be surprised if the friendly owners drop off some organic fruit or freshly baked bread.

Hahei and Hot Water Beach are both a short drive away.

The Church COTTAGE $$
(☏ 07-866 3533; www.thechurchhahei.co.nz; 87 Hahei Beach Rd; cottages $140-215; ☏) 🐾 Set within a subtropical garden, these beautifully kitted-out, rustic timber cottages have plenty of character. The switched-on new owners are really welcoming and have loads of ideas on what to do and see around the area.

🍴 Eating & Drinking

The Church MEDITERRANEAN $$
(☏ 07-866 3797; www.thechurchhahei.co.nz; 87 Hahei Beach Rd; shared plates $10-28; ⊘ 5.30pm-late Mon-Sat, shorter hours outside summer) This ultra-charming wooden church is Hahei's swankiest eatery with excellent Spanish- and North African–inspired dishes made to be shared, as well as a stellar, if pricey, selection of Kiwi craft beers. Try the lamb tagine with yoghurt and couscous or the Moroccan-style steamed mussels. Booking ahead is recommended as the dining room is cosy and compact.

★ Pour House PUB
See p46

Purangi Winery WINERY, BEER GARDEN
(☏ 07-866 3724; www.facebook.com/purangiestateltd; 450 Purangi Rd; ⊘ 11am-8pm) Rustic and laid-back – almost to the point of being pleasantly ramshackle – this slightly eccentric combination of winery, beer garden and wood-fired pizza restaurant (pizzas $18 to $25) is in a rural setting 6km from Hahei on the road from Ferry Landing. Try the feijoa fruit wine, liqueur and cider, and say gidday to the friendly posse of cats usually mooching around.

Cathedral Cove

Hot Water Beach

Famous for its hot water at low tide, Hot Water Beach is also popular with surfers, who stop off before the main beach to access some decent breaks. The headland between the two beaches still has traces of a Ngāti Hei *pa* (fortified village).

🏃 Activities

Hot Water Beach Store OUTDOORS
See p45

🛏 Sleeping & Eating

Hot Water Beach
Top 10 Holiday Park HOLIDAY PARK $
(☑07-866 3116; www.hotwaterbeachholidaypark.com; 790 Hot Water Beach Rd; campsites from $23, dm $30, units $90-180; @ 🛜) 🏊 Bordered by tall bamboo and gum trees, this is a very well-run holiday park with everything from grassy campsites through to a spacious and spotless backpackers lodge and stylish villas with arched ceilings crafted from NZ timber.

Hot Waves CAFE $$
(☑07-866 3887; 8 Pye Pl; mains $12-26; ⊙8.30am-4pm Mon-Thu & Sun, to 8.30pm Fri & Sat) In summer everyone wants a garden table at this excellent cafe. For a lazy brunch, try the eggs Benedict with smoked salmon or a breakfast burrito. It also hires spades for the beach ($5). Ask about occasional Friday-night music sessions.

Whangamata

POP 3560

When Auckland's socially ambitious flock to Pauanui, the city's young and free head to Whangamata to surf, party and hook up. It's a true summer-holiday town, but in the off-season there may as well be tumbleweeds rolling down the main street.

🏃 Activities

The **Wentworth Falls walk** takes 2½ hours (return); it starts 3km south of the town and 4km down the unsealed Wentworth Valley Rd. A further 3km south of Wentworth Valley Rd is Parakiwai Quarry Rd, at the end of which is the **Wharekirauponga walk**, a sometimes muddy 10km return track (allow 3½ to four hours) to a mining camp, battery and waterfall that passes unusual hexagonal lava columns and loquacious bird life.

SurfSup OUTDOOR SPORTS
See p46

Kiwi Dundee Adventures TRAMPING
(☑07-865 8809; www.kiwidundee.co.nz) 🏃 Styling himself as a local version of Crocodile Dundee, Doug Johansen offers informative one- to 16-day wilderness walks and guided tours in the Coromandel Peninsula and countrywide.

🛏 Sleeping

Wentworth Valley Campsite CAMPGROUND $
(☑07-865 7032; www.doc.govt.nz; 474 Wentworth Valley Rd; adult/child $10/5) 🏊 More upmarket than most DOC camping grounds, this campsite is accessed from the Wentworth Falls walk and has toilets, showers and gas barbecues.

Breakers MOTEL $$
(☑07-865 8464; www.breakersmotel.co.nz; 324 Hetherington Rd; units $165-240; 🛜🏊) Facing the marina on the Tairua approach to Whangamata, this newish motel features an enticing swimming pool and spa pools on the decks of the upstairs units.

🍴 Eating & Drinking

Soul Burger BURGERS $
(☑07-865 8194; www.soulburger.co.nz; 441 Port Rd; burgers $11-16; ⊙5pm-late Wed-Sun) Serving audacious burgers with names like Soul Blues Brother and Vegan Vibe, this hip corner joint is also licensed so you can have an ice-cold beer with your burger.

Argo Restaurant MODERN NZ $$
(☑07-865 7157; www.argorestaurant.co.nz; 328 Ocean Rd; mains $28-33; ⊙5.30-9.30pm Thu-Sun & 9am-2.30pm Sat & Sun, daily late Dec-early Feb; 🛜) Whangamata's most stylish restaurant offers a concise menu of innovative bistro classics including garlic-infused linguine with Coromandel mussels, and fish with a black rice risotto and a curry coconut sauce. The starter of pork belly croquettes goes well with a hoppy IPA, and the airy deck is perfect for a few lazy afternoon drinks.

SixfortySix CAFE $$
(☑07-865 6117; www.facebook.com/sixfortysix whangamata; 646 Port Rd; mains $10-26; ⊙7.30am-11pm) Rightly lauded as one of regional NZ's better cafes, SixfortySix does tasty counter food like baguettes crammed with hoisin pulled pork, as well as more substantial mains including spicy fish tacos

and a great scallop and bacon burger. New Zealand wine, local craft beer from Coromandel's Hot Water Brewing Co and freshly squeezed juices and smoothies join good coffee on the drinks menu.

Lincoln   PUB
(☑07-865 6338; www.facebook.com/thelincoln whangamata; 501 Port Rd; ⊙5pm-late Sun-Fri, 9am-late Sat) Part pub, part bistro, part cafe and all-round good times feature at this versatile spot on Whangamata's main drag. DJs kick in on summer weekends.

ℹ️ Information

Whangamata Info Plus (☑ 07-865 8340; www. thecoromandel.com/whangamata; 616 Port Rd; ⊙9am-5pm Mon-Fri, 9.30am-3.30pm Sat & Sun) Staffed by a friendly and well-informed team.

Waihi & Waihi Beach

Waihi's main drag, Seddon St, has interesting sculptures, information panels about Waihi's golden past and roundabouts that look like squashed daleks.

The *Historic Hauraki Gold Towns* pamphlet (free from the Waihi i-SITE) outlines walking tours of both Waihi and Paeroa.

👁 Sights

Gold Discovery Centre   MUSEUM
See p46

Athenree Hot Springs   SPRING
(☑07-863 5600; www.athenreehotsprings.co.nz; 1 Athenree Rd, Athenree; adult/child $7/4.50; ⊙10am-7pm) 🏊 In cooler months, retreat to these two small but blissful outdoor hot pools, hidden within a holiday park.

Waihi Arts Centre & Museum   MUSEUM
(☑07-863 8386; www.waihimuseum.co.nz; 54 Kenny St, Waihi; adult/child $5/3; ⊙10am-3pm Thu & Fri, noon-3pm Sat-Mon) The Waihi Arts Centre & Musuem has an art gallery and displays focusing on the region's gold-mining history. Prepare to squirm before the collection of miners' chopped-off thumbs preserved in glass jars.

🏃 Activities

Goldfields Railway   RAILWAY
(☑07-863 8251; www.waihirail.co.nz; 30 Wrigley St, Waihi; adult/child return $18/10, bikes $2 extra per route; ⊙departs Waihi 10am, 11.45am & 1.45pm Sat, Sun & public holidays) Vintage trains depart

Waihi for a 7km, 30-minute scenic journey to Waikino. It's possible to take bikes on the train so they can be used to further explore the Karangahake Gorge section of the Hauraki Rail Trail. The timetable varies seasonally so check the website.

Waihi Bicycle Hire   BICYCLE RENTAL
(☑07-863 8418; www.waihibicyclehire.co.nz; 25 Seddon St, Waihi; bike hire half-/full day from $30/40; ⊙8am-5pm) Bike hire and loads of information on the Waihi end of the Hauraki Rail Trail.

🧭 Tours

Waihi Gold Mine Tours   TOUR
See p47

🛏 Sleeping

**Bowentown Beach
Holiday Park**   HOLIDAY PARK $
(☑07-863 5381; www.bowentown.co.nz; 510 Seaforth Rd, Waihi Beach; campsites from $46, units $85-195; @🛜) Having nabbed a stunning stretch of sand, this impressively maintained holiday park makes the most of it with first-rate motel units and camping facilities.

**Waihi Beach Top 10
Holiday Resort**   HOLIDAY PARK $
(☑0800 924 448; www.waihibeachtop10.co.nz; 15 Beach Rd, Waihi Beach; campsites from $29, units $120-214; @🛜🏊) This massive, resort-style holiday park is pretty darn flash, with a pool, gym, spa, beautiful kitchen and a smorgasbord of sleeping options.

Westwind B&B   B&B $
(☑07-863 7208; westwindgarden@xtra.co.nz; 58 Adams St, Waihi; s/d $50/90) Run by a charming couple who are inveterate travellers themselves, this old-fashioned homestay B&B has two comfortable rooms with a shared bathroom.

Waihi Beach Lodge   B&B $$$
(☑07-863 5818; www.waihibeachlodge.co.nz; 170 Seaforth Ave, Waihi Beach; d $295) A short stroll from the beach, this boutique accommodation features colourful, spacious and modern rooms as well as a studio apartment with its own kitchenette. Legendary breakfasts are often served on a sunny deck. Ask the friendly owners Greg and Ali how they're going with their homemade honey and limoncello,

and hopefully look forward to sampling both.

Manawa Ridge
LODGE $$$

(☏07-863 9400; www.manawaridge.co.nz; 267 Ngatitangata Rd, Waihi; r $950) The views from this castle-like ecoretreat, perched on a 310m ridge 6km northeast of Waihi, take in the entire Bay of Plenty. Made of recycled railway timber, mudbrick and lime-plastered straw walls, the rooms marry earthiness with sheer luxury.

✖ Eating

Boy Oh Boy
CAFE $

(www.facebook.com/boyohboy; 28 Wilson Rd, Waihi Beach; snacks $6-8; ⊙6am-4pm) Caffeine-infused cosmopolitan style comes to Waihi Beach at this sunny rustic cottage with loads of outdoor seating. Other tasty diversions include top fruit smoothies, and wholemeal pies and calzones. Vegan and organic influences also abound in Waihi Beach's smallest and friendliest cafe.

Waihi Beach Hotel
BISTRO $$

(☏07-863 5402; www.waihibeachhotel.co.nz; 60 Wilson Rd, Waihi Beach; mains $20-32) Auckland restaurateurs the Hip Group helped to inspire the excellent local dining scene when they took over this classic Kiwi hotel in 2014. The versatile menu runs from ricotta hotcakes with lemon curd and mascarpone for brunch to a terrific beef burger with hand-cut chips for dinner. Relaxed sophistication inspires the service and there is an excellent wine and craft beer selection.

Don't miss the adjacent store dispensing great coffee, the North Island's best gourmet sausage rolls and delicious ice cream (try the salted caramel).

Flatwhite
CAFE $$

(☏07-863 1346; www.flatwhitecafe.co.nz; 21 Shaw Rd, Waihi Beach; mains brunch $14-20, dinner $20-35; ⊙8am-late; 🛜) Funky, licensed and right by Waihi Beach, Flatwhite has a lively brunch menu, decent pizzas and flash burgers. A recent makeover has added huge decks with brilliant ocean views. Our favourite off the new dinner menu is the blackened salmon with a chargrilled corn and saffron salsa.

Porch Kitchen & Bar
CAFE $$

(www.theporchwaihibeach.co.nz; 23 Wilson Rd, Waihi Beach; mains brunch $14-35, dinner $28-35; ⊙8am-late) Resurrected as an even better restaurant after a fire, Waihi Beach's buzziest combo of cafe and bar serves sophisticated and substantial mains. Kick off with macadamia crumbed scallops for lunch, or return at night for grilled chicken with a spicy chipotle harissa and garlicky gourmet potatoes.

ℹ Information

Waihi i-SITE (☏07-863 9015; www.waihi.org. nz; 126 Seddon St, Waihi; ⊙9am-5pm, to 4pm winter) Local information and the interesting Gold Discovery Centre (p46), a modern and interactive showcase of the gold-flecked past, present and future of the Waihi region.

Driving in New Zealand

New Zealand crams diversity into its island borders, and road journeys seamlessly combine ocean-fringed coastal roads, soaring alpine peaks and impressive glaciers.

Driving Fast Facts

➡ **Right or left?** Drive on the left

➡ **Manual or automatic?** Mostly automatic

➡ **Legal driving age** 18

➡ **Top speed limit** 100km/h

➡ **Best bumper sticker** 'Sweet as bro'

DRIVING LICENCE & DOCUMENTS

International visitors can use their home country driving licence, or an International Driving Permit (IDP) issued by their home country's automobile association. If their home country licence is not in English, they must also carry an approved translation of the licence. See www.nzta.govt.nz/driver-licences.

INSURANCE

Rental car companies include basic insurance in hire agreements, but it's often worth paying an additional fee – usually on a per day basis – to reduce your excess. This will bring the amount you need to pay in case of an accident down from around $1500 or $2000 to around $200 or $300. Note that most insurance agreements won't cover the cost of damage to glass (including the windscreen) or tyres, and insurance coverage is often invalidated on beaches and certain rough (4WD) unsealed roads. Always read the fine print, ask pertinent questions, and definitely refrain from driving a rental car along Ninety Mile Beach, Northland.

HIRING A CAR

Hiring a vehicle is very popular in NZ, and the country is perfect for self-drive adventures. Most – but not all – rental car companies require drivers to be at least 21 years old. The main companies are all represented; the following are good-value independent operators with national networks.

Ace Rental Cars (☏09-303 3112, 0800 502 277; www.acerentalcars.co.nz)

Apex Car Rentals (☏03-363 3000, 0800 500 660; www.apexrentals.co.nz)

Go Rentals (☏09-974 1598, 0800 467 368; www.gorentals.co.nz)

Also very popular is renting a campervan and taking advantage of the Department of Conservation (DOC) network of campsites. The following are three well-regarded local companies.

Apollo (☏09-889 2976, 0800 113 131; www.apollocamper.co.nz)

Jucy (☏09-929 2462, 0800 399 736; www.jucy.co.nz)

Road Trip Websites

AUTOMOBILE ASSOCIATIONS

New Zealand Automobile Association (www.aa.co.nz/travel) Provides emergency breakdown services, maps and accommodation guides.

CONDITIONS & TRAFFIC

New Zealand Transport Agency (www.nzta.govt.nz/traffic) Advice on road works, road closures and potential delays.

ROAD RULES

Drive Safe (www.drivesafe.org.nz) A simplified version of NZ's road rules, with the information of most interest to international visitors.

New Zealand Transport Agency (www.nzta.govt.nz) Search for 'Road Code' for the full version of NZ's road rules.

Maui (☏09-255 3910, ☏0800 688 558; www.maui.co.nz)

Another option is to contact **Transfer-car** (☏09-630 7533; www.transfercar.co.nz), one-way relocation specialists for car rental.

BUYING A VEHICLE IN NEW ZEALAND

Buying a car and then selling it at the end of your travels can be one of the cheapest ways to see NZ.

➡ Auckland is the easiest place to buy a car, followed by Christchurch. **Turners Auctions** (www.turners.co.nz) is NZ's biggest car-auction operator, with 10 locations.

➡ Make sure your prospective vehicle has a Warrant of Fitness (WoF) and registration valid for a reasonable period: see **New Zealand Transport Agency** (www.nzta.govt.nz) for details.

➡ Buyers should take out third-party insurance, covering the cost of repairs to another vehicle resulting from an accident that is your fault: try the **Automobile Association** (AA; ☏0800 500 444; www.aa.co.nz/travel).

➡ To have a car inspected before you purchase it (around $150), see **Vehicle Inspection New Zealand** (VINZ; ☏09-573 3230, 0800 468 469; www.vinz.co.nz) or the AA.

➡ To establish if there's anything dodgy about the car (eg stolen, outstanding debts), try the AA's **LemonCheck** (☏09-420 3090, 0800 536 662; www.lemoncheck.co.nz) service.

BRINGING YOUR OWN VEHICLE

As NZ is an island nation, it is extremely rare for travellers to bring their own vehicle to the country. One exception where it could be financially worthwhile is for Australian visitors who are planning on travelling in their own campervan or caravan. Search for 'Importing a Vehicle Temporarily' on www.nzta.govt.nz.

MAPS

➡ Excellent national and regional maps published by the **New Zealand Automobile Association** (www.aa.co.nz) are available free of charge at regional i-SITEs (tourist information centres) and at main international airports. Also free and available at i-SITEs are regional maps and guides published by **Jasons** (www.jasons.co.nz).

➡ More detailed maps including street and topographic information are published by **Land Information New Zealand** (LINZ; www.linz.govt.nz).

➡ The Automobile Association also has a good online Travel Time and Distance Calculator to plan driving routes around NZ.

ROADS & CONDITIONS

➡ Kiwi traffic is usually pretty light, but it's easy to get stuck behind a slow-moving truck or a line of campervans. Be patient.

➡ One-way bridges, winding routes and unsealed gravel roads all require a more cautious driving approach.

➡ Carry tyre chains with you if you're travelling in alpine areas or over high passes during autumn and winter.

➡ If you stop for a photo, pull well over to the left and ensure your vehicle is not in the way of traffic.

Road Distances (km), North Island

	Auckland	Cape Reinga	Hamilton	Napier	New Plymouth	Paihia	Rotorua	Taupo	Tauranga	Thames	Waitomo Caves
Cape Reinga	430										
Hamilton	125	555									
Napier	420	860	300								
New Plymouth	360	790	240	410							
Paihia	225	220	340	645	590						
Rotorua	235	670	110	220	300	460					
Taupo	280	720	155	140	300	505	80				
Tauranga	210	635	110	300	330	435	85	155			
Thames	115	540	110	360	340	345	170	210	115		
Waitomo Caves	200	620	75	300	180	420	165	170	150	175	
Wellington	640	1080	520	320	350	860	450	375	530	590	460

➡ Distances on the map can be deceptive as narrow roads are often slower going than expected. Allow enough time for travel, and in more remote areas, ask at local petrol stations about the road ahead.

➡ Animal hazards often include farmers moving herds of cows or flocks of sheep. Slow your vehicle to a crawl – you may need to stop altogether – and patiently let the animals move around your car.

➡ Because of Auckland's geographic location, squeezed into a narrow coastal isthmus, rush hour motorway traffic from 7am to 9am and 4pm to 7pm can be very slow. If possible, try to avoid heading north or south out of the city around these times.

ROAD RULES

The full version of New Zealand's road code can be found on www.nzta.govt.nz, but here are the basics:

➡ Drive on the left, overtake on the right.

➡ Safety belts (seat belts) must be worn by the driver and all passengers. Younger children must be secured in an approved child seat (these can be rented from rental-car companies).

➡ Motorcyclists and their passengers must always wear helmets.

➡ When entering a roundabout (traffic circle), always give way to the right.

➡ Come to a complete halt at STOP signs.

➡ The speed limit is 100km/h on motorways and the open road, and usually 50km/h in towns and cities. Always drive to the conditions and reduce speed if it is raining, windy or icy.

➡ For drivers over 20 years of age, the legal alcohol limit is 50mg of alcohol per 100mL of blood. This equates to around one to two standard drinks, but as different people process alcohol differently it is recommended that drivers should not drink at all. In NZ, drivers under the age of 20 cannot legally drink any alcohol if they are planning on driving.

➡ Driving under the influence of drugs is strictly illegal.

PARKING

Finding a car park gets easier – and substantially cheaper – out of Auckland, but

Road Distances (km), South Island

	Blenheim	Christchurch	Dunedin	Franz Josef Glacier	Greymouth	Invercargill	Kaikoura	Milford Sound	Nelson	Picton	Queenstown	Te Anau
Christchurch	310											
Dunedin	665	360										
Franz Josef Glacier	500	390	560									
Greymouth	330	250	550	180								
Invercargill	870	570	210	530	710							
Kaikoura	130	185	535	540	330	745						
Milford Sound	1060	760	410	630	805	275	930					
Nelson	115	425	775	470	290	990	245	1100				
Picton	30	340	690	530	355	900	160	1090	120			
Queenstown	785	480	285	355	530	190	660	290	820	815		
Te Anau	945	640	295	515	690	160	815	120	980	975	170	
Timaru	465	165	200	490	350	410	340	605	580	495	330	490

locations around key attractions definitely get very busy during peak periods.

➡ In city centres, most on-street parking is by 'pay and display' tickets available from on-street machines.

➡ Timing for paid parking is usually from 9am to 6pm Monday to Saturday with free parking on Sundays. This does vary in larger urban centres, however, so always check times carefully.

➡ Cash is needed for machines in provincial towns, but most city machines can also be paid by credit card or by smartphone.

➡ Most expensive is central Auckland, with costs up to $6 per hour from Monday to Friday. Prices are usually cheaper on weekends.

➡ See www.wilsonparking.co.nz for locations of paid multistorey and underground car parks in Auckland, Hamilton, Wellington, Christchurch, Queenstown, Invercargill and Dunedin.

➡ Yellow lines along the edge of the road indicate a nonparking area, and drivers should also be aware of 'loading zones', which can only be used by commercial vehicles for short time periods.

➡ Clamping of vehicles is not very common in NZ, but council parking wardens and tow-truck drivers strictly enforce local parking rules – tow-away warnings should definitely be taken seriously.

FUEL

➡ Fuel is readily available throughout the country.

➡ See www.aa.co.nz/cars/motoring-blog/petrolwatch for current petrol and diesel prices.

➡ Fuel prices are generally cheaper in cities than in provincial areas.

➡ Most supermarkets offer fuel discount vouchers with shopping purchases over $40; check your docket.

SAFETY

➡ Driving in NZ is generally a hassle-free experience, but it is not unknown for rental cars and campervans to be targeted by opportunistic thieves.

➡ Always keep baggage and valuables locked in the back of the vehicle, out of sight. When parking in unattended car parks in popular tourist spots, consider carrying passports, money and other valuable items with you while you are away from your vehicle.

➡ If you have just arrived in the country after a long international flight, it is strongly recommended that you have a re-energising overnight stay in your city of arrival before getting behind the wheel on NZ roads.

➡ **DriveSafe** (www.drivesafe.org.nz) is an excellent online resource – published in English, French, German and Chinese – for international drivers on NZ roads.

DOC CAMPSITES & FREEDOM CAMPING

A great option for campervan travellers are the 250-plus vehicle-accessible 'Conservation Campsites' run by the Department of Conservation (www.doc.govt.nz). Fees range from free (basic toilets and fresh water) to $15 per adult (flush toilets and showers). Pick up brochures detailing every campsite from DOC offices and i-SITEs or see online.

New Zealand is so photogenic, it's often tempting to just pull off the road and camp for the night, but there are strict guidelines for 'freedom camping'. See www.camping.org.nz for more freedom-camping tips.

➡ Never assume it's OK to camp somewhere: always ask a local or check with the local i-SITE, DOC office or commercial camping ground.

➡ If you are freedom camping, treat the area with respect and do not leave any litter.

➡ If your chosen campsite doesn't have toilet facilities and neither does your campervan, it's illegal for you to sleep there (your campervan must also have an on-board grey-water storage system).

➡ Legislation allows for $200 instant fines for camping in prohibited areas or improper disposal of waste (in cases where dumping waste could damage the environment, fees are up to $10,000).

RADIO

New Zealand is well-covered by radio, and national station networks can be listened to on different frequencies around the country. Check each network's website for the relevant frequency in various areas of the country.

Driving Problem-Buster

What should I do if my car breaks down? Call the service number of your car-hire company and a local garage will be contacted. If you're travelling in your own vehicle, join the New Zealand Automobile Association; they can attend to breakdowns day and night. Another option is Motoring 24-7 (www.roadside-assistance.co.nz).

What if I have an accident? Exchange basic information with the other party (name, insurance details, driving licence number). No discussion of liability needs to take place at the scene. It's a good idea to photograph the scene of the accident noting key details. Call the police (☎111) if necessary.

What should I do if I get stopped by the police? They will want to see your driving licence, and a valid form of ID if you are visiting from overseas. Breath testing is mandatory in NZ.

What if I can't find anywhere to stay? Try to book ahead during busy periods. Local i-SITEs can often help with last-minute accommodation bookings.

Will I need to pay tolls in advance? New Zealand has three toll roads: the Northern Gateway Toll Road north of Auckland, and the Tauranga Eastern Link Toll Road and the Takitimu Drive Toll Road, both in Tauranga. Tolls are specific to a vehicle's registration number and can be paid online at www.nzta.govt.nz or at Caltex and BP service stations. Tolls can be paid either prior to travel, or within five days of travelling on a specific toll road.

Cruising Cook Strait

On a clear day, sailing into Wellington Harbour, or into Picton in the Marlborough Sounds, is magical. Cook Strait can be rough, but the big ferries handle it well, and distractions include cafes, bars and cinemas. Booking online is easiest; sailings can usually be booked up to a couple of days in advance. Exceptions are during school and public holidays, and from late December to the end of January. There are two ferry options:

Bluebridge Ferries (☎04-471 6188, 0800 844 844; www.bluebridge.co.nz; 50 Waterloo Quay) Crossing takes 3½ hours; up to four sailings in each direction daily. Bluebridge is based at Waterloo Quay, opposite Wellington train station.

Interislander (☎04-498 3302, 0800 802 802; www.interislander.co.nz; Aotea Quay) Crossings take three hours, 10 minutes; up to five sailings in each direction daily. Interislander is about 2km northeast of Wellington's centre at Aotea Quay.

Car-hire companies allow you to pick-up/drop off vehicles at ferry terminals. If you arrive outside business hours, arrangements can be made to collect your vehicle from the terminal car park. In some cases, it may suit the hire company for you to take your rental car with you on the ferry – eg for relocations etc – so ask them to advise what will be the best deal.

Radio New Zealand National (www.radionz.co.nz/national) News-oriented station with excellent coverage of local issues, arts and culture.

Newstalk ZB (www.newstalkzb.co.nz) Talkback station where the issues of the day are discussed passionately.

Radio Sport (www.radiosport.co.nz) Understand the difference between the All Blacks, Black Caps and Silver Ferns (respectively NZ's national rugby, cricket and netball teams).

Hauraki (www.hauraki.co.nz) Iconic rock music station with a quintessentially irreverent Kiwi tone.

BEHIND THE SCENES

SEND US YOUR FEEDBACK

We love to hear from travellers – your comments help make our books better. We read every word, and we guarantee that your feedback goes straight to the authors. Visit **lonelyplanet.com/contact** to submit your updates and suggestions.

Note: We may edit, reproduce and incorporate your comments in Lonely Planet products such as guidebooks, websites and digital products, so let us know if you don't want your comments reproduced or your name acknowledged. For a copy of our privacy policy visit lonelyplanet.com/privacy.

ACKNOWLEDGMENTS

Climate map data adapted from Peel MC, Finlayson BL & McMahon TA (2007) 'Updated World Map of the Köppen-Geiger Climate Classification', *Hydrology and Earth System Sciences*, 11, 163344.

Cover photographs: Front: Road leading to Oneroa Bay, Bay of Islands, David Wall/Alamy©; Back: Overlooking Auckland from Mt Eden, Ian Trower/AWL©

THIS BOOK

This 1st edition of *Auckland & the Bay of Islands Road Trips* was researched and written by Brett Atkinson and Peter Dragicevich. This guidebook was produced by the following:

Destination Editor Tasmin Waby

Product Editor Alison Ridgway

Senior Cartographer Diana Von Holdt

Book Designer Virginia Moreno

Assisting Editors Bruce Evans, Anne Mulvaney

Assisting Cartographers Corey Hutchison

Assisting Book Designers Michael Buick, Katherine Marsh, Wendy Wright

Cover Researcher Naomi Parker

Thanks to Grace Dobell, Andi Jones, Catherine Naghten, Kirsten Rawlings, Kathryn Rowan

OUR STORY

A beat-up old car, a few dollars in the pocket and a sense of adventure. In 1972 that's all Tony and Maureen Wheeler needed for the trip of a lifetime – across Europe and Asia overland to Australia. It took several months, and at the end – broke but inspired – they sat at their kitchen table writing and stapling together their first travel guide, *Across Asia on the Cheap*. Within a week they'd sold 1500 copies. Lonely Planet was born.

Today, Lonely Planet has offices in Dublin, Franklin, London, Melbourne, Oakland, Beijing and Delhi, with more than 600 staff and writers. We share Tony's belief that 'a great guidebook should do three things: inform, educate and amuse'.

INDEX

000 Map pages